UNIQUE EATS AND EATERIES OF SONOMA COUNTY

THE PEOPLE AND STORIES BEHIND THE FOOD

YVONNE MICHIE HORN

REEDY PRESS

Reedy Press
PO Box 5131
St. Louis, MO 63139, USA
www.reedypress.com

Library of Congress Control Number: 2022937108

ISBN: 9781681064123

Design by Jill Halpin

Photos by author unless otherwise noted.

Printed in the United States of America
22 23 24 25 26   5 4 3 2 1

UNIQUE EATS AND EATERIES

OF

SONOMA COUNTY

THE PEOPLE AND STORIES BEHIND THE FOOD

YVONNE MICHIE HORN

Gravenstein Apples
Courtesy Sonoma County Tourism

DEDICATION

To those who call Sonoma County home,
and to those who come to visit.

CONTENTS

ACKNOWLEDGMENTS

What would Sonoma County do without the newspaper food writers who keep their fingers on the pulse of the area's eating scene? Thank you *Santa Rosa Press Democrat*'s Diane Peterson, features; Heather Irwin, dining editor; and writers Carey Sweet, Jeff Cox, and Michele Anna Jordan. And thank you Houston Porter, *Argus Courier* food section writer, for keeping watch on Petaluma's extremely lively and diverse eateries; and to you, Kathleen Hill, *Sonoma Index Tribune*, for covering the town of Sonoma.

Sonoma County Tourism's media gallery of food images proved beyond helpful, and everyone, not just writers, should give a round of applause for SCT's *Life Opens Up* online presence.

To the family and friends who cheered me on, came up with "unique eats and eateries" suggestions to help fill the list of 84 the book called for, and agreed to come with me on dining adventures—I owe you! But most of all, thank you Sonoma County for the bounty of the county, so blessed by Mother Nature, and to the independent farmers and ranchers who tirelessly supply the incredible products that fuel our tables.

Crane Melons
Courtesy Sonoma County Tourism

INTRODUCTION

What fun to write *Unique Eats and Eateries of Sonoma County*! After all, who doesn't like to sit down and listen to a good story? Especially when it's accompanied by good food, as was I while listening to chefs, restaurant owners, and producers of farm-fresh eats relate the why, what, and where tales of their being.

It was exciting when someone told me about an eatery that I should check out, especially so when it turned out to have great food, a fascinating story, and that special something about it that made it unique. Along the way, interesting commonalities emerged like the number of chefs whose love of cookery began in their mom's or grandmother's kitchen.

The writing of this book came on the heels of the successful 2021 launching of *100 Things to Do in Sonoma County*, both Reedy Press's guidebook series titles. A travel writer, my wings remained clipped by the ongoing pandemic, allowing me, a third-generation resident of the county, to take on another book, this time an in-depth look at one facet of this bountiful and beautiful place in the world I call home—its food.

Famed early 20th-century horticulturist quote about Sonoma County said it well: "The chosen place of all this earth as far as nature is concerned, here anything can grow." Vineyards produce world-class wines, fabulous fish is pulled from the sea, small independent farmers till the soil to harvest a year-round abundance that finds its way into restaurant kitchens. It all works together to make Sonoma County a fabulous place to eat, as you will see as you turn the pages and eat your way through the pages of this book. Bon appetit!

Mac's Deli & Café
Courtesy Mac's Deli & Café

UNIQUE EATS AND EATERIES OF SONOMA COUNTY

DUNGENESS CRAB

Gift from the sea

The entire county holds its breath as the calendar turns to November. Will there be Dungeness crab for Thanksgiving dinner? Delays in the commercial catch are duly reported in the local papers—the possibility of tardy migratory whales becoming entangled in the gear; algae bloom lingering in the sea; fishermen and wholesalers wrangling over the price per pound; dangerous seas. Eating Dungeness crab isn't exclusively a Sonoma County tradition, but those who live there consider it so.

Dungeness crab gets its name from a fishing village on Washington State's Olympic Peninsula where the species was first commercially fished in 1848. Crab pots are now set from Alaska to Baja, California. Bodega Bay fishermen, however, say their crabs are larger and sweeter than anywhere else due to summer sea temperatures and plentiful food sources. "Crabs shipped in from Oregon or Washington aren't the same," a longtime local fisherman says. "Knowing that the crab you're eating was pulled out of the water less than 24 hours ago is really special."

Not for the faint of heart is buying crab live off the boat at Bodega Bay's Spud Point Marina. Choose the liveliest. Take courage and plop it into a big pot of salted boiling water. You'll hear some scratching about, but don't take off the lid. Keep the pot boiling for 15 minutes or so.

Purists insist that the season's first crabs should be eaten neat, with just a squeeze of lemon, leaving garlic-laden melted butter and tomato-based seafood sauces for crabs to come. And it should be a social thing, enjoyed in a messy cracking-and-picking gathering around the table.

Top left: *Crabs await cracking*

Above left: *Fishermen set their crab traps*

Above center: *Tony Anello boils crab at the family's Spud Point Crab Co.*

Top right: *Dungeness crab straight off the boat*

Above right: *Live crabs for sale, right off the boat. All photos Sonoma County Tourism*

Two styles of eating have emerged. Some people crack open the shells, pick out the succulent meat, and eat it as they go. Others crack the shell and pile the crab up into a magnificent Dungeness feast—all while each style looks jealously at the other.

It's an oh-so-Sonoma County thing to do.

Spud Point Marina
1818 Westshore Rd., Bodega Bay, 707-875-3535

In most years, Dungeness crab season runs roughly mid-November through March.

TUDOR ROSE ENGLISH TEAROOM

Tea without the stuffy

Mary Poppins pops in, to the delight of a roomful of dressed-for-the-occasion kids and their "mums" for an afternoon of "Supercalifragilisticexpialidocious" and other irrepressible-nanny tunes. Interspersed is tea-time etiquette instruction: back straight, napkin on your lap, no elbows on the table, little finger extended as you lift your teacup. Poppins popping in is just one of the scheduled events at Tudor Rose, from holiday teas to murder mystery nights. "Traditional English with a twist" is how Angela Grant describes her tearoom.

You can, of course, come simply to enjoy dainty triangular sandwiches (white bread, no crusts), little cream puffs, cookies, scones, and preserves arranged on tiered doily-lined plates. Endless cups of tea are poured. Or choose the Henry VIII steak and Guinness pie, the Duchess Kate salad of organic mixed greens, or the Winston Churchill chicken potpie for lunch or dinner.

Grant, born and raised in Liverpool, is English through and through, minus any idea of the English as stuffy. While traveling through the moors of Devon, she happened upon a cottage offering tea and stopped for what she describes as the most memorable tea experience of her life. Then and there she knew that opening a tearoom was what she wanted to do. But why Santa Rosa and not

Tudor Rose sources its 18 different teas from the Duncans Mills Tea Shop, which specializes in teas, spices, and tea ware.

Left: *Top tier tea offering. Photo courtesy Tudor Rose*
Top right: *Tudor Rose entrance. Photo courtesy Yvonne Horn*
Center right: *Done up for a private tea party. Photo courtesy Tudor Rose*
Above right: *Cups ready for teatime. Photo courtesy Tudor Rose*

England? That story is too long to relate here; ask her and she'd be pleased to share.

For two years before her tearoom's 2013 opening, Grant haunted thrift and antique shops in search of furnishings, fine china, linens, and quintessential English art objects. With these finds, she produced an interior that is both elegant and welcoming but not a bit stuffy. Expect Grant to greet you as "love" or "dear" when you walk in the door. "I couldn't be stuffy if I tried to," she says.

733 Fourth St., Santa Rosa, 707-535-2045
tudorrosetearoom.com

AQUS CAFÉ

Building a sense of community

Stop by in the morning, order a latte, and choose an irresistible pastry. Settle in on the flower-filled deck in the shade of a red umbrella and peruse the monthly events schedule, a listing of more than 60 intriguing options: trivia nights, poetry readings, discussions of community concerns, musical jam sessions, newcomer-to-town gatherings, and more.

In the early 1990s, Irishman John Crowley arrived in Petaluma and established a flourishing software design company. As the years passed, the town became as dear to him as the Dublin he'd left behind. But he felt that something was missing, something akin to the Irish pubs long operated by his grandfather, father, uncle, and brother, where everyone felt welcomed as part of the shared community—teachers, construction workers, the parish priest.

In 2006, Crowley opened Aqus Café Foundry Wharf as a place for people from all walks of life to find common ground, create friendships, engage in meaningful conversations, and realize a sense of belonging. The café hosted fun and inspiring gatherings to draw people in, along with excellently prepared food emerging all day from the café's kitchen.

In Aqus's light and airy space, works by local artists hang on the walls, rotating through children's efforts to those of well-regarded professionals. Music happens on most nights—jazz,

"I like to think that Aqus has had an impact on Petaluma." –Owner John Crowley, summing up the café's 15-plus years of existence

Top left: *Umbrella-shaded exterior. Photo courtesy Yvonne Horn*

Top center: *Aqus salad. Photo courtesy Aqus Café*

Top right: *John Crowley. Photo courtesy Aqus Café*

Center left: *Music Night. Photo courtesy Aqus Café*

Center right: *Caprese panini. Photo courtesy Aqus Café*

Above: *Order at the counter. Photo courtesy Yvonne Horn*

swing, folk, bluegrass, and of course Celtic. If you're wondering whether "Aqus" has some obscure Irish meaning, it doesn't. Crowley just liked the sound of it.

189 H St., Petaluma, 707-778-6060
aqus.com

EL MOLINO CENTRAL

Mexican cookery from scratch

El Molino's brightly painted exterior on the corner of Highway 12 and Central Avenue in Boyes Hot Springs will draw you in. Eat there once and you'll be back time and time again. The cuisine is described as Mexican street food brought to its zenith, but it's more than that. From the restaurant's small kitchen come dishes—traditionally cooked at home—that are prepared with the best and freshest of ingredients.

Owner and chef Karen Taylor Waikiki's love affair with Mexican cuisine began 40 years ago, when she became immersed in cooking authority Diana Kennedy's book, *The Cuisines of Mexico*. Inspired, she went to Oaxaca to learn from Kennedy, and they became friends. For a number of years, Waikiki cooked at a Mexican restaurant in the town of Sonoma, working side by side with immigrants from various parts of Mexico and learning from them. In 2010, she opened El Molino Central with a menu based on traditional Mexican cookery.

Traditional food at El Molino Central begins with masa, the cornmeal basis for so many dishes. Here it is made from scratch. Raw corn kernels are soaked in alkaline water and ground in a mill (hence the name El Molino) to produce a soft, wet dough that results in fresh, rich-tasting tortillas unlike those you've carried home from the supermarket.

Waikiki continues to learn from her employees, most of them women who have emigrated from Mexico, collaborating on new dishes and giving them credit on the menu. Recently, Juanita's chicken chalapas with avocado and Rufina's pork tamales appeared.

As it has been since El Molino's opening day, you order at the register and then walk past the kitchen and through the

Top left: *Final touch from the kitchen. Photo courtesy Sonoma County Tourism*
Above left: *Karen Taylor, El Molino Central proprietor. Photo courtesy John Storey*
Top right: *Red umbrella shaded benches for patio dining. Photo courtesy Yvonne Horn*
Above right: *Enchiladas. Photo courtesy El Molino Central*

screen door to the green-painted picnic tables shaded by red umbrellas out back. Try not to fill up on stone-ground chips and salsa as you wait; your chile rellenos, chicken mole enchiladas, wild halibut ceviche, or whatever you ordered will soon be arriving through the screen door.

11 Central Ave., Sonoma, 707-939-1010
elmolinocentral.com

A cold case stocks ready-made items that you can carry home to your fridge.

SWISS HOTEL

Landmark dining on the Sonoma Plaza

The Swiss Hotel has seen it all. Flags on the balcony display its history: the flags of California, the United States, Switzerland, and Italy.

Don Salvador Vallejo, brother of California general Mariano Vallejo, built the handsome adobe structure around 1840 to house his growing family. As the years passed, other families called it home. Ideally situated on the north side of the town's busy plaza, it emerged as a stagecoach-stop hotel in the 1870s. In 1892, the Toroni family bought the property, naming it the Ticino Hotel in remembrance of Switzerland's southernmost canton, from which they hailed. When the hotel on the far side of the plaza burned to the ground, the Toronis found its sign intact, appropriated it, and—voila!—the Ticino Hotel became the Swiss. It has been so ever since.

Why the Italian flag? Hank Marioni is the fourth generation of his family to own and operate the restaurant-hotel. His great-grandfather Mose Mastelotto bought it in 1923, passing it on through a succession of sons and daughters to Marioni's ownership in 1991.

Inside, walk into the bar and you'd swear nothing has changed since 1923. Take time to peruse the gallery of historic photographs hanging on the walls. Beyond, the dining room provides a crisp-white-linen dining experience. Out back, the patio garden's red-

The Swiss Hotel shares the north side of the plaza with Sonoma State Historic Park's buildings.

Top left: *Porch out front is the place to dine on warm-weather days. Photo courtesy Sonoma County Tourism*

Above left: *Bar area is filled with photos of past Swiss Hotel days. Photo courtesy Swiss Hotel*

Top right: *General Vallejo's bronze likeness relaxes on a bench across the street from what was once his brother's house. Photo courtesy Yvonne Horn*

Above right: *Patio dining. Photo courtesy Sonoma Plaza*

checked tablecloths emphasize the restaurant's largely Italian menu; pizzas emerge from a wood-burning oven.

The place to see and be seen on balmy days and evenings is out front on the porch beneath the flag-flying balcony—red-checked tablecloths again. Unending entertainment comes in the form of people-watching, courtesy of the plaza's passing parade of mostly tourists. The Vallejo brothers would be amazed.

18 W Spain St., Sonoma, 707-938-2884
swisshotelsonoma.com

DRY CREEK PEACH

Going, going—saved!

Vineyards carpet seemingly every inch of the Dry Creek Valley's 16-mile length and 2-mile width. Signposts at crossroads bristle with winery names. The valley is best known for its zinfandel, and grape-growing has been going on in the valley for nearly a century and a half. But tucked away among the valley's sea of vines is a surprising treasure, Sonoma County's only remaining peach orchard.

San Franciscans Gayle Okumura Sullivan and her husband, Brian Sullivan, stumbled upon the orchard in 2000 while looking for a piece of land, a country home where they might grow "something"—the something to be decided on when the property was found. What they found was ready made: a farm of peach trees along with a smattering of other stone fruits.

In vineyard-abundant Dry Creek, it was expected that the Sullivans would tear out the orchard in favor of grapes. Instead, they planted 100 more peach trees and dedicated themselves to the more than 60 years of organic farming practiced by the orchard's previous owner.

Thirty varieties of peaches, both white and yellow, provide fruit for harvesting throughout the season, roughly late April into September, each lasting a couple of weeks. Red Haven, "a classic peach that's almost old-fashioned," starts off the parade; Last Chance, "deeply colored and simply beautiful," marks the finale.

Excess peaches find their way into jars of jam, each batch redolent of the variety from which it is made.

Top left: *Gayle Okamura Sullivan (right) and Brian (left)*

Above left: *30 varieties of peaches are planted.*

Top right: *Picked peaches are packed in single layers.*

Above right: *Excess fruit is made into jam. All photos courtesy Dry Creek Peaches*

Fruit is handpicked firm-ripe, sorted by hand, and boxed in a single layer. "Labor intensive," sum up the Sullivans.

Look for the Sullivans' peaches at the Healdsburg and Santa Rosa Original farmers markets. The farm stand on the Dry Creek property is open on most Wednesday, Saturday, and Sunday afternoons throughout the season. Call ahead to make sure they are open.

2179 Yoakim Bridge, Healdsburg, 707-433-8121
drycreekpeach.com

CAFÉ FRIDA GALLERY

Art, music, coffee, and food

A chunk of historic Santa Rosa was left behind in the late 1940s, when Highway 101 cut through the city. Out of sight and mind, the once vibrant area slowly descended into downright "iffy."

It is now known as the South of A Street Art District. The turnaround developed gradually as, one by one, artists found affordable space in forgotten commercial and industrial buildings. Today, the tree-shaded street is home to some 40 art studios and galleries, along with enticing one-of-a-kind shops.

Café Frida Gallery, named for Mexican painter Frida Kahlo, is a recent addition. True to the neighborhood's quirky ambiance, you'll miss the place unless you're paying attention to a long driveway leading to the café's art-filled patio. The co-owners are Mario Uribe and his son-in-law Mamadou Diouf. Uribe was an early contributor to Santa Rosa's arts scene and an early proponent of the district; don't miss his gallery, Sei Shen, on mural-packed Art Alley, its name reflecting Uribe's schooling in traditional Japanese art. Diouf, who is originally from Senegal, has more than 20 years of culinary and hospitality experience.

Uribe had long felt that a hangout for the street's artists, shop owners, and visitors was missing from the neighborhood. The two envisioned a place for art, music, and of course, excellent coffee and food: a café marrying Diouf's African and French heritage with Uribe's Hispanic and Asian perspective.

How did the café get its name? In 2018, Uribe "just for fun" painted a large tableau picturing Mexican artist Frida Kahlo and her husband, Diego Rivera, with famed Sonoma County horticulturist Luther Burbank. Kahlo and Burbank never met, but from photos obtained from Burbank's widow Kahlo produced a portrait of Burbank rooted in the ground that now resides in the

Top left: *Café Frida co-owners, Amadou Diouff (left) and Mario Uribe (right). Photo courtesy Becky Stender*

Above left: *Artistically arranged dishes emerge from the kitchen. Photo courtesy Café Frida*

Top right: *Urife's painting of Frida Kahlo, Diego Rivera, and Luther Burbank hangs in the café's interior. Photo courtesy Cafe Frida*

Above right: *Café's airy and spacious interior. Photo courtesy Café Frida*

Museo Dolores Olmedo in Mexico City. "In my head, I had the three of them meet and pose for me," Uribe says, "but it turned out so big that I'd no place to hang it." Space was found in the café's bright and airy interior, inspiring the café's name.

300 S A St., Santa Rosa, 707-308-4344
cafefridagallery.com

Winterblast, the art district's annual festival, features a parade of decorated couches. Why couches? S(outh) of A. Got it?

DIVINE DELIGHTS

Teeny cakes

Each can be downed in a bite or two, but what a shame! What the French call petit fours should be eaten in divine nibbles. Multiple layers of almond-butter cake filled with velvety smooth fruit and butter cream encased in frosting beg to be savored. Take your time.

Bill Fry and his wife, Angelique, entered the bakery business in 1985 selling the usual variety of breads, cakes, pastries, and cookies. Competition was fierce, however, and margins shrank. To survive, they decided to choose one item and make it irresistible. In 1990, they brought their tiny cakes to Petaluma.

Thirty-two years later, Bill Fry estimates that the company creates more than a million little cakes each year. Each travels through steps that have become increasingly automated. In one of the steps, straight out of Willy Wonka, hundreds of little cakes travel via conveyor belt on their way to becoming smoothly enrobed in chocolate.

A cadre of decorators using tiny paper piping bags then takes over to create the illusion that the little cake is a package tied up with a bow, to pretty it up with a little flower, or to pipe on a just-so squiggle. The work is precise; when packaged, pieces must be identical to one another.

Wholesale business, selling to such entities as high-end mail-order catalogs, accounts for approximately 85 percent of total sales. Petaluma residents in the know head for Divine Delights headquarters, located in an industrial park on the east side of town, to purchase a ready-made box, place a special order, or pick up a small bag of discounted petit fours that haven't passed muster. The

Top left: *Teeny cakes. Photo courtesy Divine Delights*

Above left: *Photo courtesy Divine Delights*

Top right: *Exterior, outlet store. Photo courtesy Yvonne Horn*

Above right: *Photo courtesy Divine Delights*

retail counter is open 10 a.m. to 4 p.m. weekdays. Chances are that either Bill or Angelique will be behind the counter. Despite its size, Divine Delights remains a mom-and-pop business.

1250 Holm Rd., Petaluma, 707-559-7099
divinedelights.com

GRAVENSTEIN APPLES

Sonoma's perfect apple

In 1884, world-renowned horticulturist Luther Burbank suggested to a Sebastopol rancher that Gravenstein apples would do well on his 78 acres. Early-morning fog creeps into the area from the coast, departing in time for days to turn warm—Gravenstein weather, Burbank advised. Sonoma County's commercial apple industry took off, with Gravenstein the undisputed king.

"If the Gravenstein could be had throughout the year, no other apple need be grown," Burbank commented. And he's right. With just the right balance of tart and sweet, crisp yet juicy, they are not only great for eating out of hand but also ideal for applesauce, juice, and baked goods—yum, Gravenstein apple pie!

In the 1940s, 10,000 acres of Gravenstein orchards burst into spring bloom in Sonoma County, notably in the soft hills surrounding Sebastopol. But only 704 acres remain today.

Don't jump to the conclusion that the county's proliferation of wine grapes led to the apple's near-extinction. That's only partially true. In the 1980s, apples became a prolific worldwide commodity, driving the price per ton so low that many Sonoma growers had no choice but to bow out. Delicate and perishable, unlike the supermarket-popular Red Delicious, for example, the Gravenstein does not store or ship well. Gravensteins also ripen early, at a time when people are still enjoying stone fruits and are not yet ready to think about apples; unlike other varieties, they don't ripen all at once, making harvesting difficult.

In 1811, Russian fur trappers brought Gravenstein cuttings with them to plant in the orchard of their Fort Ross colony, which is now a state historic park.

Top left: *Candied apples, a kid Gravenstein Apple Fair favorite. Photo courtesy Sonoma County Tourism/Kristen Newsom*

Above left: *Apples weighed out for purchase at annual Gravenstein Apple Fair. Photo courtesy Sonoma County Tourism/Kristen Newsom*

Top right: *Gravensteins ready for plucking. Photo courtesy Sonoma County Tourism*

Above right: *Apple cider tasting at the annual Gravenstein Appple Fair. Photo courtesy Sonoma County Tourism/Kristen Newsom*

In 2005, Slow Food USA declared the Gravenstein a heritage food and included it in its Ark of Taste catalog of endangered foods.

While thousands of acres of blossoming apple trees are not likely to be seen again in the rolling hills around Sebastopol, diversified agriculture is a hot topic in the county. Here and there, new organically farmed orchards are blossoming out. Craft ciders are coming on strong, with fresh-pressed organic Gravenstein juice a prized ingredient.

To sample a Gravenstein apple, mark your calendar. Every August, Sebastopol's Gravenstein Apple Fair celebrates its prized fruit in a weekend of old-fashioned fun; apple peeling, apple juggling, and candy-apple-eating contests are among the activities, along with apple pie judging and, of course, fresh-off-the-tree Gravenstein apples to carry home. So it has been since 1973.

gravensteinapplefair.com

CANEVARI'S DELICATESSEN

Old-school Italian

For years, to say "Canevari" was to say "ravioli"—specifically, ravioli made the traditional Italian way, with dough rolled to a just-so thickness and squares filled with a vegetable and meat mixture and plenty of garlic.

Attilio and Maria Canevari came to Santa Rosa from San Francisco in 1924. Five years later, they began to supply homemade ravioli to local markets, with a workforce composed of themselves and, one by one as they grew old enough to mince garlic and stir, their four children—Pietro, Albina, Gino, and Edwin. The business grew. Demand for the Canevaris' plump little squares expanded to markets and restaurants throughout the county.

To house the growing business, in 1939, the family built Canevari's Ravioli Factory on Lewis Road and added a delicatessen. First Pietro joined the enterprise, followed by Gino. The sales territory soared to the Oregon border.

While the deli on Lewis Road continued to hum along through the years, sales of massive amounts of ravioli gradually evaporated. In 1982, Attilio passed away. Edwin took the helm. In 2011, with no Canevari grandchildren willing to take on the family business, Edwin, then in his late 70s, reluctantly passed the torch. Lou Chambrone, whose grandparents on both sides had immigrated to the United States from Italy in the 1920s, now heads the kitchen and is behind the deli counter.

Huge ravioli-making machines–a gigantic roller and a dough mixer–stand like sculptures in the parking lot, paying homage to Canevari's ravioli heyday.

Top left: *Canevari's exterior. Photo courtesy Yvonne Horn*

Above left: *Ed Canevari as a child poses with his father Attilio. Photo courtesy Canevari's*

Above center: *Sandwich of the day. Photo courtesy Canevari's*

Top right: *Plates of ravioli follow the original recipe. Photo courtesy Canevari's*

Above right: *Old ravioli-making equipment, now parking lot sculptures, are reminders of time past. Photo courtesy Yvonne Horn*

While dedicated to carrying on the business the "right way," the Canevari way, Chambrone brought with him years of experience as a restaurant chef. Canevari's old-school Italian cuisine is now being served up in a fresh new way. Always to be found in the cold case is ravioli rolled and filled according to the original recipe.

695 Lewis Rd., Santa Rosa, 707-545-6941
canevarisdeli.com

MOM'S APPLE PIE

Forty-plus years of pies

"Betty, you make a great apple pie. Why don't you sell it?" Ever since her husband, Harry Carr, made that suggestion in 1979, Betty Carr has been turning out pies. Zillions of pies. That first pie was offered at the Carrs' roadside fruit stand on what locals call the Gravenstein Highway, officially Highway 116. Ingredients for the pie came from the Carrs' Gravenstein apple orchard on the property.

By 1984, Betty had rolled out, filled, and baked so many pies that the Carrs changed the name of their roadside business, the Hilltop, to Mom's Apple Pie. In her signature red-and-white-checkered apron, Betty became known to tourists and locals alike as the "mom" of Mom's Apple Pie. Harry, whom Betty credits as the driving force behind the business, died in 1992. "He was the Mr. Mom of Mom's Apple Pie," she says. Betty carried on.

Walk into the flower-edged, bright-yellow building today to choose from among 16 varieties of pie. Most are fruit-filled, with apple remaining the star. At Gravenstein harvest time, customers wait in line to take home a pie filled with apples from the Carrs' organic orchard. After the short Gravenstein season, Granny Smith apples and other preferred varieties take over.

Hankering for more pie? Stop by the Petaluma Pie Co. located downtown in Putnam Plaza. Metal chairs and tables outside the shop provide prime real estate for people-watching while downing a savory or sweet handcrafted pie.

125 Petaluma Blvd. N, Petaluma, 707-766-6743

petalumapiecompany.com

Top: *Come on in for pie. Photo Sonoma County Tourism*

Above left: *Tableware to take home. Photo courtesy Yvonne Horn*

Above right: *Mom's Apple Pie since 1979. Photo courtesy Yvonne Horn*

Now well into her eighth decade, Betty is no longer among those rolling out circles of pastry for the pies offered each day. Chances are, however, that you'll run into her during one of her multiple daily forays into the shop. She is, after all, still the responsible "mom" of Mom's Apple Pie.

4550 Hwy. 116 N, Sebastopol, 707-823-8330
momsapplepieusa.com

EUROPEAN FOOD STORE

Eat your way through the world

Olga Rozhkova's small grocery guarantees that foods familiar to Sonoma County's European emigrees need not be mere motherland memories. Aisles and cold cases are filled with imported items from Switzerland, Germany, Ukraine, Finland, Italy, Poland . . . On the list goes, including, of course, Olga's home country, Russia. If you're an emigree from Georgia, you might have a reunion with pine-cone jam; from France, a tin of Anis de Flavigny, tiny candy balls bursting with flavor. There are frozen bags of piroshki, ready to be taken home and dumped into a pot of boiling water. You'll also find packaged pasta and spaetzle, sausages and patés, teas and cheeses and chocolates, smoked fish, and varieties of caviar. Loaves of rye bread, ordered frozen from Germany and baked daily in the store's oven, are a best seller.

Olga and her husband, Anatoliy, came to Sonoma County from their Siberian home in 2001, leaving behind a wholesale business of, ironically, importing food products from the United States. Particularly in demand were chicken legs, the least expensive cut of the bird, which the Rozhkovas supplied in cases of hundreds. Olga, pregnant at the time, was flying back and forth to the United States to fulfill orders. The couple, concerned about the quality of medical care in Russia, concluded that it would be best for her to stay in the United States and return to Siberia after the birth. Instead, Anatoliy joined her; the family has made their home in the county ever since.

Russian friends kept suggesting that she open a grocery selling foods they missed from home. European Food Store opened in 2011, its inventory quickly expanding to embrace the entirety of Europe as customers began to ask whether she might possibly stock their longed-for this or that. "Swedish cloudberries," Olga remembers, "took three months, but I found them."

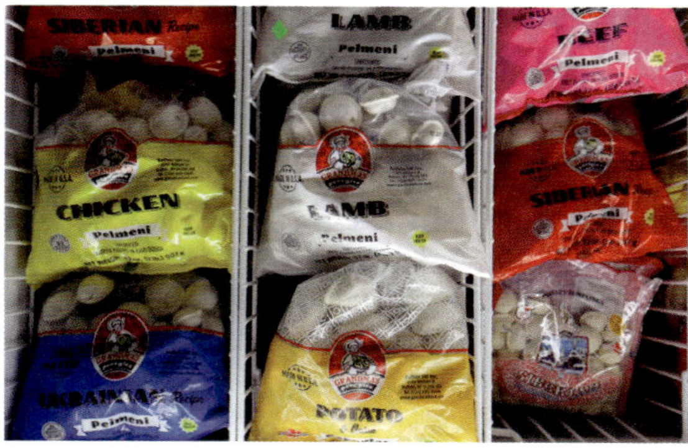

Top left: *Caviar from around the world. Photo courtesy Yvonne Horn*

Above left: *Store exterior. Photo courtesy European Food Store*

Top right: *Olga Rozhkova, store owner. Photo courtesy European Food Store.*

Above right: *Frozen bags of piroshki, ready to be taken home. Photo courtesy Yvonne Horn*

German-born Jill Schulze became a steady customer, chatting easily with whoever else was shopping. Fluent in five languages, she became the store's general manager in 2017. "Every day in the store is like traveling the world," she says.

2790 Santa Rosa Ave., Santa Rosa, 707-527-0319
europeanfoodsonoma.com

A small collection of decorative and gift items, such as Russian nesting dolls, beg to be carried home with your grocery items.

TAQUERIA MOLCAJETES

Steaming vessels of goodness

Molcajetes are the mortars and pestles utilized throughout Mesoamerica for thousands of years. Aztecs and Mayans used them, and it's the rare Hispanic household that doesn't have one in its kitchen today to grind spices and pound salsa, mole, and guacamole ingredients into age-old submission.

Tradition calls for a molcajete to be carved from a single block of volcanic stone into a squat, three-legged bowl. Over time it becomes deliciously layered with flavor from all the previous things squished in it. But it has another use, as a serving dish that keeps food hot for a long time. A pile of them in Taqueria Molcajetes's kitchen are used for just that.

Wedged in between a hair salon and the office of a cat veterinarian in a Safeway-anchored strip mall, the taqueria is not easy to find. In this tucked-away spot, co-owners Zacarias Martin, who grew up in the Mexican state of Jalisco, and Dionicia Valdovinos, a native of Michoacán, serve up an extensive menu of dishes influenced by their homeland.

Order one of the molcajetes; five are listed as house specialties. Your order will soon arrive in a molcajete heated to, as one diner put it, "the temperature of the sun." Don't think of touching it! If you ordered molcajete mixto, you'll get a steaming mix of steak,

"Without question, one of the best Mexican food experiences I've ever had." –Guy Fieri on the Food Network's *Diners, Drive-Ins and Dives*

Left: *Street view. Photo courtesy Yvonne Horn*

Top right: *Boiling hot seafood molcajete. Photo courtesy Taqueria Molcajetes*

Above right: *Molcajetes, restaurant specialty. Photo courtesy Taqueria Molcajetes*

chicken, shrimp, and vegetables with a cactus paddle (*nopale*) hanging over the edge. With the accompanying rice, beans, sour cream, and guacamole, it adds up to a lot of food. Bring along a friend, or two, to share. And take your time; a molcajete keeps things hot for nearly an hour.

1195 W College Ave., Santa Rosa, 707-544-8280

STOCKHOME

Cosmopolitan everyday eating

For a number of years, San Francisco diners enjoyed an ode to Nordic cuisine at Roberth and Andreas Sundell's elegant Pläj before heading for an opera or symphony performance steps away. When Pläj permanently closed its kitchen in 2021, the Sundells had already opened in downtown Petaluma an entirely different view of what it means to dine Scandinavian-style—Stockhome.

Instead of offering such Pläj items as grilled saddle of elk with lingonberries and juniper jus, Stockhome celebrates the popular food of Stockholm, Roberth's home city—food dished up in the streets and market halls, food that embraces Middle Eastern culinary influences. At Stockhome, falafel happily shares menu space with meatballs and gravlax. And there are pizzas, introduced in Sweden by Italian immigrants in the 1940s as a low-cost business opportunity. Other international newcomers followed suit, topping pizza crusts with their country's flavors—banana-curry pizza, Caribbean; kebab pizza, Turkey.

Andreas and Roberth, *mommar och poppar* to four children, are longtime Petaluma residents. Stockhome's opening fulfills their idea of a casual, family-friendly eatery true to chef Roberth's Swedish roots. Walk into an open room papered with cheerful, vintage Swedish wallpaper and furnished with sleek blond-wood tables flanked by surprisingly comfortable blue wire chairs.

Order at the counter; there are always new dishes to try. "*Välkommen!* Come try our Fiddle Head Fern," encouraged a sign

A space inside the restaurant offers a carefully curated mix of kitchenware, gift items, and wearable accessories.

Top left: *Meatballs. Photo courtesy New Rev Media*

Above left: *Summer salad. Photo courtesy Sonoma County Tourism*

Above center: *Glass jars of lördagsgodis (candy). Photo courtesy Yvonne Horn*

Top right: *Roberth and Andrea Sundell. Photo courtesy Stockhome*

Above right: *Kebab pizza. Photo courtesy Stockhome*

by the door one day. Don't leave without visiting the tempting, self-serve glass jars of *lördagsgodis*, literally translated as Saturday candies. It's a Swedish tradition that children are allowed candy only on Saturday, but on that day, they can eat as much of it as they like. Saturday or not, stock up!

220 Western Ave., Petaluma, 707-981-8511
stockhomerestaurant.com

WILLI'S WINE BAR

A winning concept

When Willi's opened 20 years ago, going out for dinner meant choosing soup or salad (or both), an entree, and dessert as the finale. Small-plate dining? What was that? Terri and Mark Stark answered that question with Willi's Wine Bar.

Terri grew up in San Mateo but summered in Sonoma County, where her mother's family had lived for four generations. Mark grew up in Maryland, near Chesapeake Bay. When they met, Mark was working as a chef in Seattle, and Terri as a manager of a catering firm in Palo Alto. As the friendship grew serious, Terri introduced Mark to Sonoma County. "What do we have to do to live here?" Mark asked. In 1999, they married and came to Sonoma County with a restaurant concept in mind.

When the two went out for dinner, they'd skip the soup-salad-entree-dessert routine and instead opt for several appetizers, as they were often the most interesting dishes on the menu. Their concept for a restaurant: one that would offer nothing other than appetizer-sized portions to be paired with suggested wines. Willi's Wine Bar opened in 2002 to instant acclaim.

The Starks, and Willi's followers, were devastated when a wildfire sweeping through the county in 2017 took the wine bar in its wake. Two years later, Willi's was back in a neighborhood shopping mall four miles from its original location. The concept was kept firmly in place, but with one change: a full bar was

Willi's Wine Bar is the flagship in the non-cookie-cutter, six-restaurant empire the Starks have developed through the years. See starkrestaurants.com

Top left: *Interior. Photo courtesy of Willi's/Loren Hanson*

Center left: *Frito Misto. Photo courtesy of Willi's/Loren Hanson*

Above left: *Terri and Mark Stark. Photo courtesy of Willi's/Mariah Smith*

Top right: *Chicken Under a Brick. Photo courtesy of Willi's/Loren Hanson*

Center right: *Old Willi's, burned in 2017 wildfire. Photo courtesy of Willi's/Bart Edson*

Above right: *Wild Mushroom Mac and Cheese. Photo courtesy of Willi's/Loren Hanson*

added. Diners can now enjoy a cocktail before moving on to wine paired with such plates as Moroccan lamb chops with preserved lemon couscous.

1415 Town and Country Dr., Santa Rosa, 707-526-3096
starkrestaurants.com/stark-restaurant/willis-wine-bar

CASINO BAR & GRILL

Bet on the unexpected

Who'd expect to find exceptional cuisine in a weathered white-frame building that announces itself in neon as "Casino" below a faded 7-Up sign? Step into a dim interior with creaky floors, a thicket of deer trophies, pool tables, and a jukebox ready to play past-era tunes, and the question continues to beg answering.

"Never judge a book by its cover" comes to mind. In the wee hamlet of Bodega, four miles distant from Bodega Bay, some of Sonoma County's most creative food comes from the Casino's tiny kitchen.

Built in 1874 as Goodman's General Mercantile, it later became a tavern. In 1939, Nebo Casini purchased the building and thought a play on the family name might encourage passersby to hit the brakes. Nebo's brother Art and Art's wife, Evelyn, bought him out and continued to operate the Casino as Bodega's watering hole and de facto town hall. In 1983, Art died; Evelyn—now well into her 90s—still shows up daily to tend bar.

Burgers were Casino's fare until—Evelyn remembers it as the late '80s—a local fisherman kept bragging about what a great cook he was. "He could look into an empty fridge and find a gourmet meal!" she recalls. "Then Stevie Rudolph came along," Evelyn continues. "She could cook!" But it was Mark Malicki, stepping into the kitchen in 2011, who put the place on foodies' "must brake" maps.

Malicki had long been known in the county as a peripatetic chef, opening restaurants to acclaim, abruptly closing them, and cooking in between as caterer and applauded winery chef. At the Casino, he could cook whatever inspired him that day, minus the grind of running a restaurant. "I've never been so happy!" he says.

After six years of nightly cooking, Malicki claimed Friday through Sunday; the Holly and Tali Show is in the kitchen the rest

Top left: *Casino Bar & Grill is easy to pass by on the highway through Bodega. Photo courtesy Sonoma County Tourism*

Above left: *Evelyn Casini, well into her 90s, tends bar. Photo courtesy Michael B. Woolsey Photography*

Top right: *Holly Carter (right) and Tali Aiona (left), the Holly and Tali Show, take over Casino's kitchen on weekdays. Photo courtesy Made Local/Paige Green Photography*

Above right: *Surprisingly inventive dishes emerge from the Casino's kitchen. Photo courtesy Sonoma County Tourism*

of the week. That would be Holly Carter, who turned garden harvest into astounding meals at the Occidental Arts & Ecology Center, and then-intern Tali Aiona. When the two worked together, hip-hop, singing, and jokes emanated from the kitchen. Garden interns dubbed them the Holly and Tali Show.

Hit your brakes and pull into the parking lot. Any night at the Casino is a good culinary bet.

17000 Bodega Hwy., Bodega, 707-876-3185

REDWOOD ICE ARENA'S WARM PUPPY CAFÉ

Peanuts creator's hangout

Woodstock playing defense against Snoopy in a frozen birdbath; Woodstock driving a Zamboni. And then there's Charles Schulz, creator of the entire *Peanuts* gang, wearing his Diamond Icers jersey #2.

Schulz's love affair with zooming about the ice began as a kid skating Minnesota's frozen ponds and continued unabated through the years. In 1969, he built the Swiss Alpine–inspired Redwood Empire Ice Arena, known as Snoopy's Home Ice, to house his passion; he skated there with his Diamond Icers team until his death in 2000 at age 77. In 1975, he initiated the arena's yearly Snoopy's Senior World Hockey Tournament. The Diamond Icers were among the competitors, of course. What began with a dozen teams has become the largest senior hockey tournament in the world, with as many as 1,100 skaters, many ex-NHL players, coming from all over the globe—the oldest 91. Good grief!

Snoopy's Home Ice is an everyday busy place with classes for all ages, public skating hours, figure skating, and junior hockey. Grab a table at the Warm Puppy Café; viewing of the goings-on

Snoopy's Gallery and Gift Shop, adjacent to the ice arena, carries the largest selection of *Peanuts* merchandise in the world. The Charles M. Schulz Museum is in the same complex. Along with ever-changing exhibits, you'll find a re-creation of his studio and a timeline of his life.

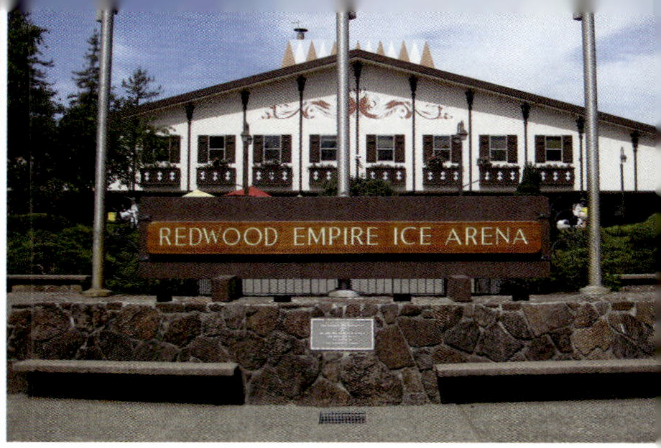

Top left: *Cartoonist Charles Schulz at his drawing board. Photo courtesy* The Guardian

Above left: *Snoopy on the ice. Photo courtesy Redwood Empire Ice Arena*

Top right: *Exterior. Photo courtesy Sonoma County Tourism*

Above right: *Warm Puppy Café. Photo courtesy Sonoma County Tourism*

can be had through wide windows alongside the rink. Be sure to order a Peppermint Patty hot chocolate. As Lucy said, "Happiness is a warm puppy."

With his studio just steps away, Schulz was a café regular, showing up daily for breakfast (English muffin with grape jelly) and lunch (tuna salad sandwich), frequently bringing a visiting cartoonist with him to discuss cartooning over lunch. A table remains reserved in his honor.

1667 W Steele Ln., Santa Rosa, 707-546-7147
snoopyshomeice.com

MITOTE FOOD PARK

Roseland's gathering place

It was a real *mitote*! Take your pick of the word's meanings: a fiesta, a celebration, an inspiration, a ruckus. On September 12, 2020, Mitote Food Park was all of the above, with a good percentage of the predominantly Latino neighborhood of Roseland showing up for a happy ruckus of music and dancing, rosary prayers, and poetry readings. Kids whacked away at a giant star-shaped piñata. Overeating was supplied by food trucks gathered for the event.

The celebration was step one in an ambitious project to turn a discarded shopping center into Roseland's vibrant, plaza-centered hub. Octavio Diaz's food truck, the Maria Machetes, which serves up classic Oaxacan recipes, was among those gathered. Diaz was selected from a group of restaurateurs to get the Mitote Food Park organized and underway as an intrinsic part of the overall project. "There's much more to come," he said.

In subsequent months, a bar fashioned from a shipping container, a stage, and a large seating area were added. Seven days a week, the trucks roll in ready to serve street food from noon to 8 p.m. or so—tacos, tamales, tlayuda, aguachile, pozole, and more. Only a certain number of trucks are permitted each day; no truck is allowed to stay more than five days a week, guaranteeing a rollover of rolling restaurants. On Tuesday and Thursday afternoons, a farmers market adds to the mitote mix.

Take your compostable container filled to the brim with whatever you've chosen—perhaps the chicken and rice plate from Diaz's truck, the chicken lovingly simmered in his mother's classic Oaxacan *mole negro*—to the tent-sheltered communal eating area, where tables are covered with brightly patterned cloths. Or eat standing up, balancing your food on one of the wine barrels placed here and there.

Top left: *Food trucks roll in on a rotating basis. Photo courtesy Yvonne Horn*

Above left: *Ceviche from the Charro Negro food truck. Photo courtesy Sonoma County Tourism*

Above center: *Mercadito offers a variety of merchandise from local vendors. Photo courtesy Yvonne Horn*

Top right: *Aquachiles, seafood ceviche. Photo courtesy Sonoma County Tourism*

Above right: *Tacos in compostable container. Photo courtesy Sonoma County Tourism*

Colorful and family friendly—Mexican music is piped in, adding to the ambiance while masking the traffic on busy Sebastopol Road—every day is a culinary mitote at Roseland's emerging and engaging gathering place.

665 Sebastopol Rd., Santa Rosa
mitotefoodpark.com

Visit the adjacent Mercadito. The vacated Dollar Tree that once anchored the property is now filled with Latino-inspired everything, from elaborate jewelry to plants in decorated pots to playthings for kids.

SOBAN

Seoul food

In times past, each member of a Korean family dined at their own soban, a small, wooden tray-like table about 12 inches high. It's a useful thing, a soban; it can also be used as a desk, as an altar, or for carrying things. Murals showing sobans in use for dining have been found in tombs dating back to the Goguryeo kingdom, 37 BC–668 AD.

You won't be required to sit on the floor at Sarah and Daniel Kim's Soban, so named as a bow to the traditional authenticity that comes out of their restaurant's kitchen. Both were born and grew up in Seoul. Daniel was 17 years old when his family immigrated to the United States. Sarah came in 2007 following their South Korean wedding.

It took a leap of faith for the Kims to open a restaurant devoted to the food of their homeland; Sonoma County, unlike the San Francisco Bay Area or Los Angeles, doesn't have a substantial Korean population. Compared to Thai, Japanese, and Chinese cuisine, Korean is an unknown. The Korean restaurant that had previously occupied Soban's location abruptly shuttered after six discouraging months. "We changed the name and menu and moved right in," Daniel says. That was in 2015.

The couple works as a team. Daniel greets and seats customers; Sarah is the chef, responsible for everything that comes out of the kitchen. Daniel brought with him 15 years of experience in restaurant hospitality, including six years at Hana, first as a server and then as front of the house. As chef, Sarah turned to the recipes she brought with her from Seoul—the cookery that the Kims enjoy at home.

Left: *Banchan, small dishes of fermented vegetables*

Top center: *Restaurant as viewed from the street*

Above center: *Sarah and Daniel Kim*

Right: *Sizzling pot of bibimbap. All photos courtesy Soban*

Bibimbap sizzles in a stone pot, as does the soondubu. Entrees arrive with banchan, small side dishes of fermented vegetables to snack on or plop atop rice. The Kims take pride in their kimchi, house-made with each ingredient fermenting under refrigeration for at least four weeks. As for Korean food's reputation as spicy, Soban is seeing an uptick in customers venturing from mild and medium toward fiery on the menu. "Spiciness is addictive," Daniel says.

255 N McDowell Blvd., Petaluma, 707-769-3112

Thanks to the popularity of Korean dramas on Netflix and YouTube, Soban is experiencing increased interest in its cuisine.

CRANE MELONS

Fifth-generation grown

Ask Jennifer Crane what makes the melons grown on her family's farm for nearly 125 years so special, and the answer will be "terroir." If you take a seed from a Crane-grown melon and plant it somewhere else, she claims, it will not produce a melon with the same unique flavor as the one farmed in the certain style, in the particular soil, and in the specific climate zone of the pioneer family's Crane Canyon ranch.

The terroir Jennifer speaks of was once part of a vast Mexican land grant that her great-great-grandfather Richard Hope Crane purchased in 1852. In time, he passed the land on to his son Oliver. In the 1920s, Oliver crossed several different varieties to develop the melon carrying the Crane name and began to sell it out of what has become known to passersby on the Petaluma Hill Road as the Melon Barn. So it has continued, with fifth-generation Rick and his sixth-generation daughter Jennifer farming the land today.

Sonoma County's jewel of sweet melons—each averaging four to seven pounds, with aromatic, light-orange, succulent flesh—is picked daily when vine-ripened-ready and delivered to the Melon Barn from around September 1 through October. Call ahead; supply on any given day may be limited.

4935 Petaluma Hill Rd., Santa Rosa, 707-795-6987
cranemelonbarn.com

Top left: *Crane melons on the vine. Photo courtesy Sonoma County Tourism*

Above left: *Jennifer Crane poses in a pile of melons for sale in the barn. Photo courtesy Yvonne Horn*

Above center: *September into October, melons are sold in the 1868 built barn. Photo courtesy Farm Trails*

Top right: *Crane family ready to tour the family ranch. Photo courtesy Crane family*

Above right: *Crane Melon Barn sign on Petaluma Hill Road. Photo courtesy Crane family*

The Crane Melon Barn, a Sonoma County Historic Site, was built entirely out of redwood in 1868 and was originally used for sheltering livestock and storing hay. When not in use for melons, the barn is a popular wedding and events venue.

FROZEN ART

A family tradition

If you're thinking of Jorge Alcázar's frozen snacks-on-sticks as "popsicles," that doesn't do them justice. These are handcrafted jewels created from fresh natural fruits and flavors—strawberry, watermelon, peach, mango, rose petal, and lavender—created in small batches of no more than 30. Throughout Mexico they're known as paletas. To Jorge they are a family tradition.

In the early 1940s, his great uncles, Ignacio and Luis Alcázar, returned to their hometown of Tocumbo, Michoacán, from a trip to the United States with the idea of using local, fresh fruit to make two categories of "ice pops," cream-based and fruit-based. Their shop was so successful that they opened a second in Mexico City. When Rafael Alcázar, Jorge's father, entered the business, franchises known as Paleteria La Michoacana had begun their spread throughout Mexico. Today the icy treats have achieved Mexican national food status.

Jorge, aged 21 in 2010, was working in Sonoma County as manager of a Mexican restaurant, aiming to set aside enough money to make a return to Mexico possible and continue the family business. "It was not just that I was next in line," he says. "It's what I've always wanted to do." At the same time, he'd come to realize that he really didn't want to leave Sonoma County. His father, who in the 1980s had operated a La Michoacana shop in

Frozen Art also creates ice cream in 42 different flavors. There are no additives or added colorings, only fresh, natural ingredients.

Left: *Frozen Art exterior. Photo courtesy Yvonne Horn*

Top right: *Frozen jewels. Photo courtesy Frozen Art*

Above right: *Art Jorge with father Rafael Jorge. Photo courtesy Frozen Art*

Sacramento, approached him with the suggestion that he open the business, not in Mexico, but where he wanted to be. Frozen Art sold its first paleta on a hot August day in 2011. Business was brisk and remains so today, with Jorge's sister Arlene Alcázar helping to run the place.

As for Tocumbo, population 1,800, the town proudly proclaims itself the birthplace of the frozen treat with a sculpture of a large globe covered with ice cream cones enclosed in a gigantic paleta.

500 Sebastopol Rd., Santa Rosa, 707-331-2899
frozenarticecream.com

BETTY'S FISH & CHIPS

Icelandic cod meets pie

Betty's has been a landmark on Highway 12 seemingly forever—"forever" being since 1967, when its original owner opened it under her first name. After a few years, Betty (her last name lost in time) sold the business, after which it was sold, and sold again and again and again, until 1996, when the Corso family bought it. Since then, Susan Corso, her son Brian, and her daughter-in-law Lori have run the restaurant as Betty's Fish & Chips, its name unchanged from 1967 to this day.

When the Corsos bought it, Betty's was in need of interior and exterior brightening. Today it's a tidy, cottagey building with metal troughs filled with flowering plants flanking the entry. Inside, decor takes note of the sea—mirrored portholes, a metal whale hanging from the ceiling, and banquettes covered in map-of-the-world's-seas upholstery.

While fish and chips—Icelandic cod enclosed in a crunchy crust—tops the menu, appetizer and sandwich offerings have been added through the years. Sauces and dressings are homemade, as are the pies. Pies?

When the family bought the restaurant, cheesecake was the sole dessert. Susan considered that a bad fit with fish. Something lemony would be much better. Modifying a basic recipe, she spread a mixture that included fruit from the family's Meyer lemon tree on a flaky crust and topped it with an impressive mound of whipped cream crowned with a slice of lemon. Voila! Lemon Cloud Pie.

So successful was the Lemon Cloud that Susan began to add other pies—apricot, apple, strawberry, boysenberry, and rhubarb (raspberry-peach won first place at the Sonoma County Fair)—all rolled out, as is the crust for the Lemon Cloud, into circular, individual portions. "I created a monster for myself," Susan laughs,

Top left: *Betty's Fish & Chips exterior. Photo courtesy Yvonne Horn*

Above left: *Signature Lemon Cloud Pie. Photo courtesy Betty's Fish & Chips*

Above center: *Betty's interior takes note of the sea. Photo courtesy Betty's Fish & Chips*

Top right: *Lori Corso behind the ordering counter. Photo courtesy Betty's Fish & Chips*

Above right: *Classic Icelandic cod fish and chips. Photo courtesy Betty's Fish & Chips*

referring to the 250 pies turned out each week. Of them, Lemon Cloud has become so famous that some customers come in for just the signature pie.

Brian credits each member of the family taking on key operating areas for the restaurant's continuing success: Brian oversees all happenings in the kitchen, Lori is the friendly and welcoming presence at the ordering counter, and Susan is the one making all those pies.

4046 Sonoma Hwy., Santa Rosa, 707-539-0899
bettysfishandchips.com

Dogs are welcome in the outside dining area. Water and dog-friendly cookies are provided.

ABYSSINIA

Tasty fun

Cooking is something girls are expected to learn how to do in Ethiopia. That was so with Wodeyelesh Merso. Women who become exceedingly good cooks are looked upon with prestige. But Wodi, as she is known, had other goals for her life. Although she married early and had a child to raise, she started a successful career in Addis Ababa.

In the early 1990s, with civil war racking the country, the family sought asylum in the United States. Sixteen years later, Wodi found herself in California in need of a job. Running a restaurant was not on her list—until she came upon an irresistible deal, a small restaurant for sale in downtown Santa Rosa. Abyssinia (the historical name of northern Ethiopia and southern Eritrea) served its first meal in 2008, with Wodi thinking "perhaps just for a year or so." She's still at it as chef with her son, Dawit Asfaha, as co-owner. "I love cooking," Wodi says. "And I get to introduce my culture and my country to other people."

In Ethiopia, diners sit on a low stool, or *berchuma*, around an hourglass-shaped basket table, or *mesob*. A server comes with a pitcher of warm water and a basin for the rinsing of hands. A large circle of *injera*—a light and airy flatbread made with the nutritious teff grain unique to Ethiopia—arrives on a plate the size of the

If you're new to the cuisine, the Abyssinia and vegetarian combos provide a good introduction.

Left: *Chef Wodi Merso, left, with co-owner and son Dawit Asfaha, right. Photo courtesy Abyssinia*

Right: *Injera topped with meat and vegetables. Photo courtesy Abyssinia*

table. On it are placed piles of what you've ordered. Diners tear off a piece of the "tablecloth," mop up a portion of food, and pop it in their mouth.

At Abyssinia, your order arrives at conventional tables lined up on either side of the shoebox-shaped eatery. On the menu are *kitfo*, beef stir-fry traditionally served as a tartare but that can be ordered medium or well done; *we't*, vegetarian or meat stews; and *tibs*, meats stir-fried with vegetables—all to be mopped up with a torn-off piece of injera. Flavors are Ethiopian-spice-market complex. Everything is delicious, and the eating, best as a shared experience, is downright fun.

913 Fourth St., Santa Rosa, 707-568-6455
my-abyssinia.com

BODEGA BAY OYSTER Co

Icy bins of mollusks

Not far from where his Irish immigrant great-great grandparents ran dairy cattle, grew potatoes, and raised eight children in the 1850s, Martin Strain farms shellfish in the waters of Tomales Bay. What began with a five-acre lease from the California Department of Fish and Wildlife in 1985 has grown to 92 leased aquacultural acres in the north, middle, and south ends of the bay.

While Strain's great-great-grandparents were working the soil, San Francisco's booming gold rush population was slurping down oysters as everyday food. So great was the demand that Atlantic oysters were seeded and farmed alongside San Francisco Bay's abundant natives. By 1910 the once-flourishing industry was dead. Changing conditions in the bay and pollution had taken their toll.

In the 1930s, pristine Tomales Bay's tidal influx of plankton-rich and temperate sea water beckoned, the same ideal shellfish-farming conditions in which Strain operates today.

One does not just fling baby oysters into the water and come back later to scoop them up. Seeds, about the size of grains of rice, are purchased from a hatchery, placed in mesh bags, and attached to long lines that enable them to rise and fall with the tides. There they stay, periodically being moved into larger bags to give them room as they grow. Depending on variety and desired size, readiness for harvesting can take six months to a year or more.

Strain operated solely as a wholesaler for many years until a roadside watering hole not far from Bodega Bay came up for sale. With his grown children, Lindsey and Whittaker ("Whitt"), now part of the enterprise, the family bought what had been known as the New Amsterdam and opened it for retail sales in 2014 as the Bodega Bay Oyster Co.

Top left: *Bodega Bay Oyster Company exterior. Photo courtesy Yvonne Horn*

Above left: *Fanciful birds in a boat float against a wall in the picnic area. Photo courtesy Yvonne Horn*

Top right: *Oysters on the half shell with all the trimmings. Photo courtesy Sonoma County Tourism*

Above right: *Son Whitt, left, and daughter Lindsey, center, joined their father Martin, right, in the family business. Photo courtesy Bodega Bay Oyster Company*

Icy bins contain Kumamoto, Atlantic, and Miyagi oysters; Manila clams; and Gallo mussels for carrying home. Step into the adjoining café for an oyster tasting and a menu that includes what might well be one of the best clam chowders on the coast.

12830 Valley Ford Rd., Petaluma, 707-876-3010
bodegabayoyster.com

On summer weekends, head for the picnic grounds out back for barbecued oysters and oysters fresh-shucked for slurping down.

PANIZZERA MEAT CO

Old school meets new ways

Redwood-covered hillsides push down on either side of two-block-long Occidental, leaving little room for expansion and even less room to park, especially on weekends. So it has been since the early 20th century, when the hamlet became known as an overeater's paradise. Italian family fare dominated. No menus. Diners, it was assumed, would catch on when platters of antipasti, tureens of soup, and tangles of spaghetti were plopped down in front of them. And, oh, those garlicky zucchini fritters!

In recent years, other eateries have found space in Occidental, making the picturesque town even more of an eater's getaway. Panizzera Meat Co. has fueled it all for more than 100 years.

Constante Panizzera arrived in Occidental from Italy with little more than sausage recipes in his pocket. In 1914, he opened Panizzera Meat Co., which he later passed on to his son Joe and, in turn, Joe's son Bob.

After 60 years of butchery, Bob was ready to retire, but no fourth-generation Panizzera waited in the wings. Enter Ryan Taylor who, with a food science degree and restaurant experience, was in Occidental tending bar while figuring out his life's next chapter. Bob often stopped by to talk food. Josh Cerda, born and raised in Occidental and working as a firefighter with the Occidental Fire Department, was well-known to Bob. Might the two become apprentices? In 2014, Panizzera Meat Co.'s 100-year anniversary, Bob turned the business over to Taylor and Cerda.

The two introduced the company to a new level of old-school butchery. Beef, lamb, heritage pork, and chicken are locally sourced. Twenty-two different kinds of sausages are made; the Italian is true to Constante's recipe. Innovations include importing Himalayan

Top left: *Ribs on the grill. Photo courtesy Panizzera Meat Co.*

Above left: *Ryan Nelson, left, and Josh Cerda, right, Panizzera Meat Co. co-owners since 2014. Photo courtesy Panizzera Meat Co.*

Top center: *Panizzera exterior. Photo courtesy Yvonne Horn*

Top right: *Constante Panizzera in his butcher shop 1920. Photo courtesy Panizzera Meat Co.*

Above right: *Cuts of beef dry-aging in Himalayan salt. Photo courtesy Yvonne Horn*

rock salt for the dry-aging of cuts, as well as a website offering shipped-to-your-door subscriptions. Panizzera meats increasingly appear on restaurant menus and in select meat counters throughout the county and beyond. Constante would be amazed.

3905 Main St., Occidental, 707-874-9770
panizzerameatco.com

STRONG ARM FARM

Low tide's nutritious gift

Tide charts let us know when creatures left behind in rock-edged pools will be on view—anemones, starfish, hermit crabs, and colorful nudibranchs. And then there's Heidi Herrmann, who considers tide charts her work schedule. When tides are at their lowest, she heads for the coast to harvest seaweed.

Negative tides, the lowest of the low, which occur during the last weeks of May through July, reveal a bounty of California's 640 species of seaweed. While anyone can wade in and carry home up to 10 pounds, Herrmann is one of only 30 licensed as an edible forager by the state and the sole holder to harvest Sonoma County's 55 miles of coastline. A good harvesting day nets 150 to 200 pounds.

A small group of volunteers will be with her—perhaps interested students from the Sustainable Agriculture class she teaches at Santa Rosa Junior College, those from her Native Plants in Restoration class at Sonoma State University, chef friends curious about the source of a cookery ingredient, or grocery owners wanting to know more about the product they carry on their shelves.

Of the 640 species, Herrmann harvests only five. Of them, wakame's golden-green strips—Japanese seaweed salad's prime ingredient—grow farthest out on the rocks. Only during extreme low tides can the foragers count on cutting and packing it into the mesh bags they carry.

But every low-tide level promises something: pungent and crunchy sea lettuce, used in salads and soups; kombu, the base for Japanese broth; nori, used in sushi; and bladderwrack, foraged primarily for its high iodine content. All are nutritional powerhouses, jam-packed with more vitamins and minerals than any plant grown in soil. Care is taken to harvest sustainably, cutting inches from the seaweed's hold on a rock so it will continue to grow.

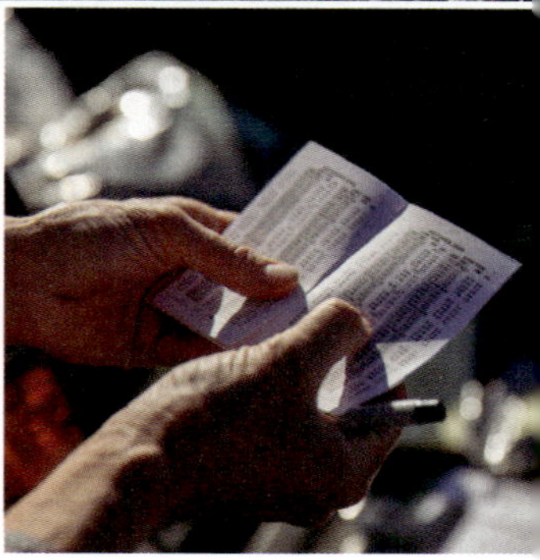

Left: *Heidi Herrmann. Photo courtesy Strong Arm Farm*

Top center: *Packaged seaweed, nutritional powerhouses. Photo courtesy Strong Arm Farm*

Above center: *Seaweed readied for drying in the sun. Photo courtesy Strong Arm Farm*

Top right: *Foragers at low tide. Photo courtesy Strong Arm Farm*

Above right: *Tide charts are Herrmann's work schedule. Photo courtesy Paige Green*

Back from harvesting, the seaweeds are cut into manageable pieces, washed and rewashed to remove grains of sand, and placed on large screens to dry in the sun. Going from colorfully sea-wet to crispy and dark takes about 12 hours. Herrmann sells her nutritious gift from the sea through Strong Arm Farm's website, to select grocers, and to restaurant chefs throughout the county and beyond.

strongarmfarm.com

Through Forage SF, Heidi Herrmann leads public tours for a fee. She instructs and informs but doesn't forage for Strong Arm Farm. Participants can take up to 10 pounds home.
foragesf.com/seaweed-foraging-sonoma

HANSON OF SONOMA DISTILLERY

Organic all the way

Vodkas are traditionally made from fermented grains and potatoes. Hanson's begin with organically grown grapes. That's step one. What follows is a long and complicated process involving a made-for-the-task pot imported from Germany and a second still imported from Cognac, France. The end result is a vodka with the subtle flavor of the grape intact. Sonoma County is wine country, after all.

But Hanson doesn't stop there. Locally grown organic fruits and vegetables, peeled and hand cut, are macerated in the original vodka in a farm-to-bottle infusion unique in the industry—cucumber, Meyer lemon, mandarin orange, and habanero. Other flavors are made seasonally—pink grapefruit, boysenberry, and ginger. Flavorings, while subtle, shine through, creating a base for craft cocktails or to enjoy straight up.

Chris and Brandon Hanson thought up the idea of a family distillery. Chris had studied distillation, and Brandon was working as a mixologist. Might their parents support them in a venture? Scott and Judy Hanson, art gallery owners, jumped on board. With two other siblings, Darren and Alanna, taking on roles, Hanson became a true family enterprise with Chris as master distiller.

Ceja Vineyards, Hanson's source for organic grapes, has a tasting room in the same complex.

Top left: *Spirit Garden table setting*

Above left: *The Hanson family team: Father, Scott Hanson (seated); Chris, master distiller, (upper left); Brandon (lower left); daughter, Alanna; Darren (far right)*

Top right: *Vodka tasting with a platter of oysters*

Above right: *Hanson's lakeside Spirit Garden. All photos courtesy Hanson Sonoma Distillery*

In 2018, Hanson opened for vodka sampling and vodka cocktails in an outdoor setting straight out of an art-gallery painting: the Spirit Garden. Food is part and parcel to the experience. Perhaps try a vodka tasting flight accompanied by a cheese and charcuterie board, great for sharing. Or a cocktail paired with pizza from the wood-fired oven, or with a platter of Hog Island oysters.

Organic grapes, organic fruits, organic vegetables—Hanson vodka must be downright healthy!

22985 Burndale Rd., Sonoma, 707-343-1805
hansonofsonoma.com

AMY'S DRIVE THRU

Fast food on its vegetarian ear

In October 1987, Rachel and Andy Berliner awaited the birth of their first child. With Rachel on bed rest, Andy headed to their natural food grocer to find a ready-made something-or-other to stick in the oven. He returned empty handed. Rachel's mother, Eleanor Goodman, came to the rescue with a vegetarian potpie she'd created—vegetables simmered in a creamy sauce inside a flaky butter crust made from organic whole-wheat flour.

After preparing the potpie numerous times in their Petaluma home kitchen—newborn Amy in her bassinet nearby—the Berliners began to think that vegetarian potpies might be marketable. If so, what should they call their company? Rachel's mother again came up with an answer: Amy's Kitchen. Less than a year later, the Berliners were working out of a full-sized Sonoma County kitchen staffed with eight employees (counting themselves).

As baby Amy grew, so did the company. Burritos and mac and cheese were the first foods to join the potpies, followed by pizzas, soups, salads, and chilis. Even candy. In a bow to Andy's candymaker dad, Organic Andy's Dandy Candy is available in seven variations.

Twenty years after the potpie launch, Amy's Kitchen was turning out 700,000 meals a day. A decade later, with kitchens added in Oregon, Idaho, and New York, 250 different products were available in 30 countries around the world.

In July 2015, Amy's Drive Thru turned American fast food on its ear, beginning with its living green-roofed, solar-paneled appearance. All the usual fast-food suspects were on the menu—burgers, fries, shakes, pizzas, burritos—but created with Amy's

Top left: *Vegetarian pizza*

Above left: *Veggie Burger*

Top right: *Veggie Burger*

Above right: *Rachel left, Amy center, Andy right. All photos courtesy Amy's Kitchen*

vegetarian care. On opening day, customers lined up at the inside counter, and cars idled in the drive-through lane. All of the 1,000 printed menus were gone by mid-afternoon.

Most popular on that opening day was the Amy Burger—a freshly made bun, onions, lettuce, pickles, optional cheddar cheese, meatless patties, and secret sauce—and it remains so to this day.

58 Golf Course Dr. W, Rohnert Park, 707-755-3629
amysdrivethru.com

TIERRA VEGETABLES

Produce above and beyond

Stop by Tierra's farm stand for freshly picked vegetables from asparagus to zucchini grown by brother-and-sister farming team Wayne and Lee James on their 17-acre farm. Tucked in between traffic-heavy Highway 101 and bustling Airport Boulevard, among Tierra's organically grown and flavorful A to Z, you'll find an abundance of varieties not found in supermarkets' produce aisles.

The siblings have farmed together for 40-plus years, since 2002, on greenbelt acreage leased from the Sonoma County Agricultural Preservation and Open Space District. Through those years, specialties have emerged. Along with seasonal sweet corn, growing space is saved for varieties of corn destined to be dried and processed into freshly ground cornmeal for home cooks to turn out polenta, breads, tortillas, and more. As many as 50 varieties of chili peppers are planted, with dozens farmed exclusively for drying. Some 20 varieties of beans are threshed and dried, most heirloom varieties gathered from various parts of the world. Tierra's Badda beans, grown for over two centuries in Sicily and traditionally used for pasta e fagioli, were entered by Slow Food International in its Ark of Taste catalog that lists agricultural products in danger of extinction.

Biodiversity and sustainability are Wayne and Lee's guidelines as they plant seedlings grown in their greenhouse, weed by hand,

Tierra encourages customers to venture out behind the Big White Barn farm stand to take a look at where the vegetables are grown.

Top left: *As many as 50 different peppers are harvested. Photo courtesy Tierra Vegetables*

Above left: *Farm stand in restored Old White Barn. Photo courtesy Tierra Vegetables*

Top center: *Tierra's heirloom beans. Photo courtesy Tierra Vegetables*

Top right: *Vegetables A to Z. Photo courtesy Tierra Vegetables*

Above right: *Wayne and Lee in Tierra's greenhouse. Photo courtesy Paige Green Photography*

harvest, and replenish Tierra's soil with composted residue. Recycle, reuse, repurpose, and preserve. Several years ago they rescued a century-old barn on nearby property from demolition and moved it to their farm; today it's their Big White Barn farm stand and produce-readying facility. Say hello to Lee's well-mannered shelties, Oso Cloudy and BeeBee, as you come in.

651 Airport Blvd., Santa Rosa, 707-544-6141
tierravegetables.com

LA GARE

Timeless French cuisine

The ambiance is Swiss alpine—even a cuckoo clock, with beamed ceilings and stained glass windows echoing the theme. White tablecloths are freshly pressed, blue napkins are swirled just so, glassware gleams, and silverware shines. That's how it was on opening day at La Gare in 1979, and that's how it is today. The menu on opening day presented classic French cuisine—think escargots de Bourgogne, French onion soup, duck a l'orange, and filet of beef Wellington. Every entree included soup and salad. Forty-plus years later, the menu remains all but identical, including the typeface.

La Gare is now in its second generation of family ownership, with chef Roger Praplan and his sister Jacqueline Bazeley, hostess and wine-cellar caretaker, running the place.

Marco, their father, trained as a classic French chef in his native Switzerland. Arriving in the United States with his wife, Gladys Praplan, he worked in acclaimed San Francisco restaurants, all the while waiting for an opportunity to follow his dream of opening his own. A vacant lot became available in a questionable area of Santa Rosa—an area that through the years has slowly evolved into today's trendy and edgy Railroad Square. "On opening night, my father hoped for 20 covers," Roger relates, "and served 70."

Roger followed in his father's footsteps, studying first in Switzerland and then in France before taking his turn on the stoves at La Gare. The customer base, established by Marco, still consists largely of locals who come to dine with a capital D. Primed for service that is welcoming and attentive, they await the arrival of menu items prepared exactly as enjoyed before—perhaps as had their parents and grandparents. "Once I mashed the potatoes

Top left: *Chef Roger Praplan. Photo courtesy La Gare*

Above left: *La Gare, an iconic presence in Railroad Square. Photo courtesy Sonoma County Tourism*

Top right: *Escargot, classic La Gare appetizer. Photo courtesy La Gare*

Above right: *Chef Roger Praplan. Wine bar claims a restaurant corner. Photo courtesy Visit Santa Rosa*

instead of how they were remembered and didn't hear the end of it," Roger recalls. An inevitable change is pricing; on opening day, a three-course dining experience could be had for $6.40 to $10.

Increased prices notwithstanding, La Gare continues to walk away with "bests" in the *Santa Rosa Press Democrat*'s annual contest—in 2021, best dining experience, most romantic dining, and (initiated during the pandemic) best takeout.

208 Wilson St., Santa Rosa, 707-528-4355
lagarerestaurant.com

"People always want to reinvent. Readjust and stick to your vision." –Chef-owner Roger Praplan

BAGEL MILL

East Coast meets West

Glenda Dougherty—her name so apropos—grew up baking by her mother's side in the family's Sebastopol kitchen. When she left home to enroll at NYU, her mind was on media studies, not baking, even as the city's famed bagels became a morning ritual. Graduation left her feeling uncertain about her life's direction. She wasn't interested in office work, she liked working with her hands, she enjoyed baking but didn't want to go to culinary school, and she missed Sonoma County.

Everything came together in 2019 with the Bagel Mill's opening in downtown Petaluma. Dougherty makes bagels the time-tested East Coast way, but with a healthy and flavorful bow to the West Coast. No shortcuts.

"Mill" in the shop's name refers to the stone mill—viewed through a window into the bakery's working area—that grinds wheat grains into whole-wheat flour. Fresh grinding shares what coffee drinkers appreciate when they grind beans for their morning coffee: increased flavor. After grinding, the process of turning flour into a bagel takes three more days.

On the second day, sourdough starter, from a small container that must be "fed" each day to keep it alive, is incorporated into the flour and allowed to slowly ferment. On day three, the dough is

Customers can also enjoy breakfast and lunch sandwiches on a bagel of choice. Special non-bagel goodies, such as cinnamon buns and sticky pecan rolls, are available on Saturday and Sunday mornings. Line up early to get yours before they run out.

Left: *Bagel Mill owner Glenda Dougherty*

Top right: *The Bagel Mill's sleek interior*

Above right: *Twelve different flavors of bagels shelved for sale. All photos courtesy Bagel Mill*

shaped into bagels and refrigerated overnight. At the crack of dawn on day four, the bagels are boiled and baked. At 7 a.m. the Bagel Mill opens to the line of early risers waiting outside.

Flavors change from time to time, but customers can usually count on plain, poppyseed, sesame, onion, garlic, cinnamon-raisin, marbled rye, whole wheat, pizza, pesto, and everything.

212 Western Ave., Petaluma, 707-981-8010
thebagelmill.com

FRANCO AMERICAN BAKERY

North Bay's oldest established bakery

Sonoma County has no shortage of artisan bakeries. And then there's Franco American. Despite a steady supply of newcomers kneading dough into loaves, many locals would not even consider, for example, tackling the season's Dungeness crab without a crusty loaf of Franco American sourdough in hand. The company's 122 years of baking history in the county is not the sole reason for such loyalty; Franco American's sourdough bread is just, well, darn good.

Franco American began with brothers Mario and Frank Bastoni selling their bread door to door. Today, thanks to successive generations of Bastoni family ownership, it's the rare grocery store that doesn't receive daily deliveries of Franco American breads; uncounted restaurants consider it daily fare. Every week, 50,000 pounds of flour is turned into nine different types of bread in 150 different styles by 39 employees running the bakery 24 hours a day. Sourdough, made from the original starter recipe, is the mainstay.

Stop by Franco American's retail store and baking facility located in the once predominantly Italian part of Santa Rosa, now known as the West End Neighborhood and Historic District. It's the same corner building where the Bastoni brothers pulled their first loaves out of the oven. Arrive in the early morning to be

Franco American also produces 10 varieties of bread under the name Mezzaluna, including focaccia, ciabatta, and pane lievitato.

Top left: *Franco American, a corner presence for near 125 years*

Top right: *Baked in Sonoma County since 1922*

Above right: *Logo. All photos courtesy Franco American Bakery*

welcomed, as have generations of residents, by the smell of freshly baked bread. Along with loaves, rolls, and baguettes still warm from the oven, you'll find day-old treats at bargain prices. Advice from the friendly person behind the counter: "Sprinkle a little water on the top, wrap the day-old item in foil, stick it in the oven for a few minutes, and it will be as if fresh-baked today."

202 W Seventh St., Santa Rosa, 707-545-7528
francobreads.com

DRY CREEK GENERAL STORE

Valley's historic staple

Dry Creek Valley settlers rejoiced when R. H. Bagley opened his general store in 1881. No longer did one need to hitch horse to wagon and trek into Healdsburg for farming essentials and household goods. A barn dance celebrated opening day, and Bagley's store became the valley's community hub.

It remained so through the years, even as the store experienced a musical chairs of ownership. Goods and services adapted as the valley transitioned from hay and sheep with but a sprinkling of vineyards into orchards of prunes, pears, and peaches. It is now carpeted edge to edge with over 9,000 acres of vineyards and some 70 wineries. In 2000, Gina Gallo, of the famed E. & J. Gallo Winery family, bought the general store and turned it into a destination for winetasters to experience the valley and taste its wines.

Stop by and step into the valley's history along with a selection of foods prepared by chef Gia Passalacqua that takes "deli" to its zenith. Passalacqua's family arrived in Sonoma County from Italy over 150 years ago—her father still manages the 500-acre ranch purchased by his grandfather. Her deep connection to the land

Take what you've ordered and snag a seat on the porch. Feel the store's ambiance and long connection to the valley as you look out over the vineyards to the mountains beyond.

Top left: *Store exterior. Photo courtesy Sonoma County Tourism*

Above left: *Deli sandwiches brought to their zenith. Photo courtesy Dry Creek General Store*

Top center: *Bellying up in the artifact-cluttered bar. Photo courtesy Sonoma County Tourism*

Above center: *Store under 1917 ownership. Photo courtesy Dry Creek General Store*

Right: *Chef Gia Passalacqua. Photo courtesy Dry Creek General Store*

brings a farm-focused approach to seasonal offerings of stop-worthy sandwiches, soups, salads, and desserts. Many ingredients come from the abundant gardens behind the store; others are sourced from local farmers.

A slow-cooked brisket with slaw, pickled vegetables, cheddar cheese, and mayo on a soft roll is hard to pass up—as are the stuffed eggs and potato salad, both classically prepared. "Sometimes the old way is the best," Passalacqua says.

3495 Dry Creek Rd., Healdsburg, 707-433-4171
drycreekgeneralstore1881.com

MYCOPIA MUSHROOMS

Tamed from the wild

David Law and Malcolm Clark grew their first cultivated mushroom in a repurposed chicken coop in an abandoned Gravenstein apple orchard. That was in 1977. Forty-plus years later, the chicken coop is now a 4,000-square-foot facility producing nine varieties of mushrooms. Among them are the Forest Nameko, a standard miso soup ingredient; Grey Oyster, the most widely consumed mushroom in the world; and Hen of the Woods, the company's best seller. With a sister facility in Michigan, Law and Clark has become the largest producer of farmed mushrooms in the United States.

Since that first mushroom, the process has become more refined, beginning with the precise hardwood-sawdust mixture each variety needs to thrive. Polyurethane bottles are filled with the mixture and injected with the variety's mycelium. Before long the factory's shelves appear as if filled with vases of exotic flowers. Sustainability is practiced from start to finish—the polyurethane bottles are reusable, the used growth medium becomes compost prized by local farmers and wineries, and surplus mushrooms are donated to local food banks.

"No longer wild, but far from ordinary" is the company's motto. Home cooks and restaurant chefs appreciate that, unlike wild mushrooms, Mycopia's are ready to go with no washing or meticulous cleaning.

2901 Gravenstein Hwy. N, Sebastopol, 707-823-1743
mycopia.com

Left: *Small highway sign marks Mycopia's location. Photo courtesy Yvonne Horn*

Top right: *Forest Nameko mushrooms in polyurethane jars. Photo courtesy Mycopia*

Above right: *David Law, left, Malcolm Clark, right, Mycopia's founders. Photo courtesy Sonoma County Tourism*

Every Friday between 1 p.m. and 3 p.m., surplus mushrooms are offered in three-pound bags for a bargain price. Be warned: three pounds is a lot of mushrooms!

WASHOE HOUSE

Watering hole with tales to tell

A number of old saloons in the West have dated and signed dollar bills tacked on their ceilings, raising the question, "Why are they there?" Reasons for the overhead monetary carpeting include early settlers wanting to ensure they'd have a bit of money to get back home should things not pan out. Others wanted to pay ahead in case of empty pockets when they next came in. Recent additions are usually to honor a celebration or because a patron simply thought it would be fun to add to the array. Washoe House, built in 1859, claims to have started the tradition. Like a lot of things about this legendary watering hole, that might even be true.

Take your pick, any or all, of what Washoe House has claimed to be in its 150-plus years—stagecoach stop, saloon, hotel, community hall, post office, and brothel. Add eatery to the list. Through the "any or all" of its existence, Washoe House has served passersby with food of a quality fluctuating from abysmal to esteemed. Now, under new ownership since 2015, it's experiencing a high. The lunch and dinner menus feature burgers of all kinds, from buffalo to Amy's veggie; steaks and salads; and a smattering of seafood options. It's nothing that could be called fancy, but it's all tasty.

Tourists and regulars alike start coming in for breakfast at 8:30 a.m. The bartender arrives an hour later, and the place takes on its noisy, convivial bustle until 10 p.m. closing time. Take in the atmosphere at a seat in the narrow, crowded bar. In addition to the

Live music adds to the happy din on weekends.

Top: *Washoe House, at its strategically located crossroads, looks little changed since stagecoach days. Photo courtesy Sonoma County Tourism*

Above left: *Bellying up to the bar under a ceiling draped with dollar bills. Photo courtesy James Photography*

Above right: *Washoe House has welcomed travelers since 1859. Photo courtesy Yvonne Horn*

dollars on the ceiling—some brown and crumbling, others crisp and green—a museum of memorabilia hangs on the walls. One of several cheeky signs reads: "Some people call them obnoxious morons. We call them customers."

2840 Roblar Rd., Petaluma, 707-795-4544
washoe.house

THE SHUCKERY

Oysters front and center

They're the Oyster Girls—sisters Aluxa and Jazmine Lalicker. Since 2007 they've been shucking oysters at oyster parties ranging from backyard gatherings to grand winery events. In 2017, they opened the Shuckery, a seafood restaurant with an oyster bar that was quickly dubbed "the pearl of Petaluma."

Aluxa and Jazmine grew up in the Yucatán where their parents—father Mexican, mother from Oklahoma—operated a hotel in Playa del Carmen and ran sailing expeditions. Following a devastating hurricane, the family took stock and relocated to Tulsa. It was there, far from the sea, that a teenaged Aluxa, the older sister, had her first encounter with the delightful taste of a briny bivalve.

"My grandfather thought it time that I should learn how to act on a date," Aluxa recalls. "So, I bought a little black dress, grandpa picked me up in his truck and off we went and ate oysters."

Fast forward a few years with Aluxa enrolled at Sonoma State University and working part time for a kayaking outfitter on oyster-rich Tomales Bay. After a friend showed her how to shuck, she began to treat clients to beachside oyster slurping.

Perhaps she was on to something. Enlisting Jazmine, the two began to book oyster parties. Classy. Sophisticated. The sister-duo shucking oysters were a hit. Business was brisk throughout the Bay Area, yet all the while the duo tended the thought that one day they'd have a restaurant, one focused on seafood with, of course, an oyster bar.

It came together on a New Orleans vacation, a city famous for oysters and where it is the rare hotel that doesn't boast an oyster bar. In Petaluma the 1923-built, art deco, Hotel Petaluma had recently emerged renovated from years of downturn, the perfect setting for what the sisters had in mind.

Left: *Oyster Girls, Lalicker sisters Jazmine (left) and Aluxa (right) create lasting relationships with oyster farmers.*

Right: *The Shuckery, as viewed through a Hotel Petaluma window. All photos courtesy the Shuckery/Debbie Wilson Photography*

As might be expected, the oyster bar is front and center, perfectly located on the way to the dining room. Snag a seat at the bar to watch and interact with shuckers who are always pleased to share what they know about what they are offering on the half shell. Some are flown in from the east coast, others from the gulf, but most importantly those delivered from the sisters' lasting relationships with the farmers tending oyster beds in the waters of Tomales Bay.

100 Washington St., Petaluma, 94952
707-981-7891, theshuckeryca.com

Between oyster parties and the Shuckery, the Oyster Girls go through hundreds of oysters a day. Shells are sent off for recycling in San Francisco where they are used to renew oyster reefs and for other uses including the making of mortar and an ingredient in chicken feed.

GOURMET GUERNEVILLE

The chef who changed Main Street

Crista Luedtke was drawn to the Russian River in 2008. She wanted a change from her San Francisco corporate life, and the area beckoned with its long history as a vacation and recreational mecca. A Guerneville boutique hotel was up for sale; Luedtke bought the property and turned it into a chic and minimalistic hostelry, boon hotel + spa. "Boon" is what Luedtke named her rescue dog, so called because the adoption was a mutual boon—a helpful and beneficial thing—for both Luedtke and her four-legged companion.

Guerneville was in a slump, only partly due to the country's descent into recession. What the town needed, Luedtke felt, was a bit of new life. Turning to her childhood years in the kitchens of her parents' restaurants, in 2009, she opened the hip and happening farm-to-table boon eat + drink in one of Main Street's empty storefronts, its cozy dining room walls featuring silhouettes of Boon catching a Frisbee. A vegetable and herb garden of raised beds planted out back soon filled with picture-perfect, organic ingredients headed for Luedtke's kitchen. Restaurant reviewers raved.

Next she established Big Bottom Market—a gourmet grab-and-go with sandwiches and salads, plus biscuits that Oprah named as one of her Favorite Things. In 2014, Luedtke's El Barrio,

Unless you're equal to taking on Main Street in one overeating day, settle in overnight at Luedtke's boon hotel + spa or her newest venture, the historic Highlands Resort nestled among towering redwoods.

Top left: *Guerneville Main Street. Photo courtesy Sonoma County Tourism*

Above left: *Interior boon eat+drink. Photo courtesy of boon eat+drink*

Top center: *Chef Crista Luedtke. Photo courtesy of boon eat+drink*

Top right: *Food that changed Main Street. Photo courtesy of boon eat+drink*

Above right: *Produce fresh-pulled from restaurant's garden. Photo courtesy of boon eat+drink*

featuring a new take on Mexican food, found space on Main Street. In 2019, she celebrated her German heritage with Brot, a contemporary *wursthaus und bierhalle*. Guerneville found itself transformed into a foodie destination.

Other entrepreneurial eateries followed suit. The shuttered Guerneville Bank now houses Chile Pies Baking Company; Nimble & Finn's opened, serving ice cream, jams, cakes, and candy. While you're there, take in the Russian River Historical Society's exhibit of the area's early years as the vacation and recreational mecca that beckoned Luedtke to Main Street.

GLEN ELLEN STAR

Exceeding expectations

Food and wine pairing is more than a dining experience at Glen Ellen Star. Chef Ari Weiswasser's wife is Errin Benziger of Benziger Family Winery, a presence in the Sonoma Valley since 1973. Errin was born and raised in Glen Ellen. Ari is from Penn Valley, Pennsylvania, where he grew up cooking alongside his mom in the family's kitchen.

Ari and Errin met as students at the University of Colorado's Boulder campus. After graduation, Ari attended the Culinary Institute of America in Hyde Park, New York, which led to his readily finding work among Manhattan's storied eateries. Meanwhile, Errin was moving from sales at the family winery to training as Benziger's East Coast representative. The two reconnected in the city and married in 2007. Three years later, they returned to Glen Ellen, with Errin commuting to the East Coast and Ari accepting a position in the French Laundry's Napa Valley kitchen, all the while marking time until they could open a restaurant of their own.

When a Glen Ellen site became available, they jumped on it as perfect for, as they described, "an inviting, neighborhood-friendly restaurant that consistently exceeds expectations." National food media took notice. In short order, *Food & Wine* named Ari the best upcoming chef, and *Condé Nast Traveler* listed Glen Ellen Star as one of the world's best restaurants. Each year since 2015, the restaurant has been recognized with the Michelin Bib Gourmand award.

That's heady stuff for a tiny building with a façade that resembles an old-fashioned storefront. In no time at all, more seating was drastically needed; an adjacent patio was enclosed for year-round use. Even so, diners sign in at a sheltered reception stand out front.

Top left: *Chef Ari Weiswasser*

Above left: *Night time front view, Glen Ellen Star*

Top right: *Wood-fired golden beet antipasti*

Above right: *One of the Weiswasser's girls poses in Glentucky Farm truck. All photos courtesy Glen Ellen Star*

Eight seats snuggle up to the counter that faces the kitchen, an ideal spot to see what goes in and out of the restaurant's "star," the wood-fired oven. From it come artisan pizzas, the wood-fired vegetables that accompany entrees, and even dessert components—save, of course, Ari's well-loved sorbets and ice creams.

13648 Arnold Dr., Glen Ellen, 707-343-1384
glenellenstar.com

While farm-to-table has become a catchphrase, much of the produce that fuels Glen Ellen Star's kitchen grows on sunny acreage less than four miles away: Benziger Family Winery's Glentucky Family Farm, certified biodynamic since 2001.

MAC'S DELI & CAFÉ

The real deal

Depending on whose memory you tap, when Mac Nesmon's deli served up its first pastrami on rye, the booths were covered in either green or some shade of blue Naugahyde. It's understandable how such details have become murky over time; that was 1952. More than 70 years later—with the deli laying claim as the oldest continuously operating breakfast and sandwich café in Sonoma County—the booths are now upholstered in a basket-weave fabric, and tables are sleekly steel legged. Everything else is pretty much the same.

Nesmon didn't operate the deli for long. In 1955, he sold to Al and Lorraine Croup, who didn't change its name. Nor did Iraj Soltani, who bought the deli in 1970. The Soltani family has been running the place as Mac's Deli & Café ever since.

In a classic immigrant story, Iraj left Iran in 1962, took a job at an East Bay restaurant, and worked his way up from busboy to manager to eatery owner before buying Mac's. In 1976, Iraj's sister Eshi came to the United States. Azi, the youngest sister, made Sonoma County her home in 1990. In the decades that followed, Eshi and Azi shared hostess and cashier duties. Azi also baked the pies that became as popular as the Reuben.

Iraj's kids, Toraj and Tami, started working at the deli as teenagers. Toraj took over in the late 1980s and has been in charge ever since.

Although there are those who lament that pie is no longer on the menu, the cheesecake and carrot cake are pretty darn good.

Top left: *Friday morning regulars*

Above left: *Club sandwich, #22 on the sandwich menu*

Above center: *Iraj Soltani, longtime owner*

Right: *Lox Benedict, a breakfast favorite. All photos courtesy Mac's Deli and Café*

The menu remains staggeringly long, offering 47 sandwiches, beginning with the classic hot corned beef or pastrami with coleslaw and ending with shrimp, avocado, cream cheese, and sprouts. Fifteen more are grilled or charbroiled—that's where you'll find the classic Reuben. The breakfast menu is nearly as lengthy; take your time choosing, as breakfast is served from opening till the mid-afternoon closing time.

630 Fourth St., Santa Rosa, 707-545-3785
macsdeliandcafe.com

DELLA FATTORIA CAFÉ

From the farm's wood-fired oven

The bakery, the breads it bakes, and the restaurant the bakery spawned are all known as Della Fattoria, meaning "from the farm." It was so named by Kathleen and Ed Weber—and fittingly so. The farm is where Della Fattoria began: breads pulled from a wood-fired oven on an old Petaluma chicken ranch. Kathleen and Ed met as Santa Rosa Junior College students; it was Ed's German-born father who owned the farm and baked bread. Kathleen was intrigued and began to challenge her father-in-law in bake-offs. Before long, Kathleen was the hands-down winner.

As a birthday gift, her family presented her with a professionally crafted wood-burning oven. Kathleen was off and running. Fourteen weekly customers and word of mouth led to restaurants taking notice, including Thomas Keller's acclaimed French Laundry. *Bon Appétit* listed Della Fattoria as one of the top 10 bread bakeries in America; Martha Stewart stopped by for a lesson in dough shaping.

In 2003, Ed and Kathleen opened Della Fattoria Café in downtown Petaluma. Son Aaron, who had culinary training and was already known as an up-and-coming chef, took over the kitchen. Daughter Elisa came on to manage the café. From time to time, Kathleen hosted farm-to-fork "ranch dinners."

In 2016, the family began to toy with the idea of offering evening meals. When the neighboring shop became available, Della Fattoria expanded into the space. Elisa took over the decor, gathering a collection of chandeliers, artifacts from the family farm, mirrors, and furnishings—everything with a

Top left: *Fresh berry tarts. Photo courtesy Visit Petaluma*

Above left: *Fresh baked breads for sale. Photo courtesy Open Table*

Above center: *Kathleen Kennedy, now deceased, Della Fattoria's inspired baker. Photo courtesy Fresh Start*

Top right: *Café's interior eclectic interior. Photo courtesy Visit Petaluma*

Above right: *Crusty loaf of Della Fattoria bread. Photo courtesy Marin Mama Cooks*

story—to create a setting that manages to be rustic, elegant, fanciful, and comfortable at the same time. Della Fattoria served its first dinners in 2018.

In 2020, after a short illness, Kathleen passed on, leaving Della Fattoria in the loving hands of Ed, Aaron, and Elisa.

143 Petaluma Blvd. N, Petaluma, 707-763-0161
dellafattoria.com

JAM'S JOY BUNGALOW

Southeast Asia with a California vibe

Jam's Joy Bungalow started out as a pink and yellow food truck. That was followed by the addition of a hole-in-the-wall walk-up on Sebastopol's town square, prompting people to ask chef-owner Jamilah ("Jam") Nixon-Mathis, "Where's the bungalow?" It wasn't until the fall of 2021 that an actual bungalow came into being, steps away from Cotati's central plaza. A constant in all three "bungalows" are dishes inspired by the spicy, sweet, aromatic flavors of Southeast Asia—California influenced, irresistibly good.

Jam grew up in Sonoma County's hamlet of Freestone but spent summers in Louisiana with her Mexican grandmother and Creole grandfather. "I learned how to make a great pot of gumbo from my grandfather," she says. But on a shrimp farm in southern Thailand during a semester abroad, she became immersed and fell in love with Southeast Asia's cuisine, the cookery she brought with her when she returned to Northern California.

For several years, Jam worked in restaurants and as a private chef before outfitting her pink and yellow food truck to take her love affair with Southeast Asian cookery on the road.

When the walk-up "bungalow" opened in 2019, one could not help but smile at its bright blue, pink, yellow, and orange exterior, with a couple of little tables and chairs placed outside echoing the color scheme. The Cotati bungalow follows suit with Adirondack chairs on its patio painted teal, pink, and yellow and an interior that follows a jungle theme with tropical potted plants and flowery oilcloth-covered tables.

Top left: *Chef Jamilah Nixon-Mathis at her Sebastopol "bungalow" door. Photo courtesy Jam Joy's Bungalow/Denice Breaux*

Above left: *Food truck. Photo courtesy Yvonne Horn*

Top center: *Crispy rice salad. Photo courtesy Jam Joy's Bungalow*

Above center: *Cotati bungalow exterior. Photo courtesy Yvonne Horn*

Top right: *Cotati Bungalow interior. Photo courtesy Yvonne Horn*

Above right: *Pork sliders on the menu. Photo courtesy Yvonne Horn*

Whether you spoon up the rice porridge, Jok, for breakfast or snack on the crispy Go's Balls with sweet chile sauce, think of how Nixon-Mathis describes her take on Southeast Asia's cuisine: "Vibrant food for spirited people."

150 Weeks Way, Sebastopol
101 E Cotati Ave., Cotati
707-843-9001, jamsjoybungalow.com

DINUCCI'S

Family-style Italian

When the Barboni family of Occidental built the Depot Hotel in 1908, the North Pacific Coast Railroad ran past the front door. Valley Ford was a welcome whistle stop on the train's Sausalito to Cazadero run until the early 1930s, when the line was abandoned. Henry and Mabel Dinucci bought the hotel in 1939 and began to serve family-style Italian meals. When Betty and Eugene Wagner became the restaurant's owners in 1968, they saw no need to change the concept. Today, with a third generation of Wagners in charge, the restaurant remains happily captured in 1968, down to its checkerboard tablecloths.

Look about. While many old bars have dollar bills covering the ceiling, here it's plastered with abalone shells tacked up by Eugene, a reminder of when one could walk out at low tide, pry an abalone off a rock, and bring it home for dinner. As for all those Jim Beam bottles displayed on shelves throughout the bar and dining areas, they were collected by Betty. All are unopened.

An idyllic mural of Sonoma County covers an entire wall—redwood forest, a squirrel or two, deer, and a fisherman trying his luck in a pond. It's signed by Chuck Pool, a mid-20th-century itinerant artist who painted it in exchange for room and board. When artists Christo and Jeanne-Claude ran the Running Fence through the coastal area in 1976, they frequently dined at Dinucci's. The Fence is remembered in large black-and-white photos. A portrait of John Wayne presides over the back dining room, reason not remembered.

A number of tables have carved wooden signs, designating that they're for regulars—Bryan's Table, Blaine and Christine's Table—who come in for the family-style parade that begins with an

Top left: *The railroad once ran past Dinucci's front door. Photo courtesy Sonoma County Tourism*

Above left: *Basil pesto spaghetti. Photo courtesy Sonoma County Tourism*

Center: *Restaurant manager Geena Garcia-Wagner pours a drink for a customer. Photo courtesy Yvonne Horn*

Top right: *Dining room, showing a display of Betty Wagner's Jim Beam collection. Photo courtesy Sonoma County Tourism*

Above right: *John Wayne's portrait presides over the dining room. Photo courtesy Yvonne Horn*

antipasti plate paired with Franco American bread and continues through minestrone and salad. All entrees come with a side-tangle of pasta Bolognese. It's a menu that hasn't changed much since 1968, with one exception: the price.

14485 Valley Ford Rd., Valley Ford, 707-876-3260
dinuccisrestaurant.com

TASCA TASCA

LaSalette's small-plate sister

Manuel Azevedo introduced Portuguese cuisine to the county in an unpretentious building on Highway 12 just outside the town of Sonoma. He named his fledgling restaurant after his mother, Lasalette. Almost after his mother, that is. Azevedo altered her name to LaSalette, thinking that if the flavors of Portugal didn't fly, he could tweak his food toward French or Italian and the name would still fit. No need. Twenty-four years later, and long ago relocated to a quiet spot off Sonoma's plaza, chef-owner Azevedo continues to enchant with fresh takes on the traditional dishes of his native Azores. Beautifully presented dishes emerge from the kitchen; service is smooth and thoughtful. Traditional. Stylish. "A restaurant for grownups," describes LaSalette.

As LaSalette approached its 20th year, Azevedo felt a need to stretch his culinary wings. Perhaps a prix fixe experience would offer a fresh spin; customers failed to embrace the idea. A space became available steps away from the town's plaza—how about a separate restaurant, a *tasca*?

In Portugal, tascas are neighborhood eateries offering *petiscos*, small portions of what might be on a homestyle restaurant's menu. Eaters order a number of petiscos all at once, adding up to a full meal.

At Tasca Tasca, numerous choices are listed under the headings Cheese, Garden, Sea, Land, and Sweet. Choose any in a fixed-price grouping of three, five, or seven items. If dining alone, just three might fit the bill; a family gathering might put together two groupings of seven. *Caldo verde*, Portugal's national soup, is of course listed, as is *bacalhau*, crunchy-on-the-outside, creamy-on-the-inside cod cakes. Feeling adventurous? Don't pass up the

Left: *Tasca Tasca exterior. Photo courtesy Tasca Tasca/Erik Castro Photography*

Top center: *Manuel Azevedo, LaSalette and Tasca Tasca chef-owner, poses next to an enlarged family photo in Tasca Tasca's dining area. Photo courtesy Tasca Tasca/ Erik Castro Photography*

Above center: *LaSalette dining room counter seating. Photo courtesy LaSalette*

Top right: *LaSalette courtyard dining. Photo courtesy LaSalette*

Above right: *Small servings add up to a full meal. Photo courtesy Tasca Tasca/Erik Castro Photography*

braised honeycomb tripe. Everything arrives all at once, save dessert, arranged on a wooden board. Wine to sip? Move over, Sonoma County. Everything on the Tasca Tasca list is from Portugal.

Tasca Tasca
122 W Napa St., Sonoma, 707-996-8272
tascatasca.com

LaSalette
6757 First St. E, Suite H, Sonoma, 707-938-1927
lasaletterestaurant.com

Azevedo's father sold two oxen and a cow to pay for his family's 1968 passage to the United States, choosing to settle in Sonoma County because of its dairy industry. Hundreds of dairies were then operating in the county, but today there are fewer than 80.

MIYOKO'S CREAMERY

Non-dairy "dairy"

Miyoko Schinner grew up as a vegetarian. Even so, she found her fine-food taste buds buzzing when her home city of Tokyo fell into a love affair with French cuisine and its gourmet cheeses. Like many vegetarians, she struggled not to give in to these dairy-rich foods. At the same time, she began to seriously wonder whether plant-based cheeses might give the French versions a delicious and decadent run for their money.

In 2010, Schinner, who'd already made a name for herself as a vegetarian chef and cookbook author—among her books, *The Vegetarian Pantry*—began to experiment in her home kitchen. The raw-food community had nut-based cheeses that she deemed acceptable, but they struck her taste buds as having an artificial flavor. Family and friends critiqued her attempts, rating them as either on the right track or headed straight to the compost pile. Two years after her first attempts, she assembled an assortment of cheeses that she considered her best versions. Tasters applauded, some rating them as superior to the dairy versions. While experimenting, Schinner also produced a new cookbook. In 2012, she published *Artisan Vegan Cheese*, a step-by-step guide for home cooks along with recipes incorporating vegan cheeses. She began planning a production facility.

Sonoma County's deep agricultural roots date from the late 19th century, when it was known as San Francisco's market basket, and continue with its current reputation as a bountiful farm-to-table

"The taste we love, without that udder stuff."
–Miyoko Schinner

Top left: *Miyoko Schinner with plant-based cheeses*

Above left: *Workers sort raw cashews for cashew-milk product base*

Top right: *Product display board*

Above right: *Plant-based butter. All photos courtesy Miyokos Creamery*

mecca. It was in Sonoma County that in 1998, Amy's Kitchen's vegetarian potpie launched the everyday acceptance of plant-based foods. What better place for Schinner's groundbreaking creamery? In 2014, Miyoko's Creamery produced its first plant-based commercial butter and cheeses, all proudly passing the "real stuff" muster of the most stringent label scrutinizer.

Miyoko's Creamery products can now be found at some 16,000 retail stores across the nation, including such mega-stores as Costco and Trader Joe's.

2086 Marina Ave., Petaluma, 415-521-5313
miyokos.com

CAFÉ AQUATICA

Where the river and ocean meet

Café Aquatica sits on a sweet curve of Highway 1 as it enters Jenner, population 136. At the café's feet, the mouth of the Russian River opens wide to meet the sea; paddle boarders and kayakers float by. One cannot imagine a more sublime spot to be on a fair day than settled into one of the weathered Adirondack chairs assembled to take in the view.

Café Aquatica has been there for at least 20 years, its clientele largely travelers passing through on their way up or down the spectacular coast. Locals consider it a community hub: a place to catch up over one of chef-owner Rachel Kulinski's pour-over brews and a pastry or two. Everything on the menu is made in house, and Kulinski's clam chowder rivals the view as reason enough to stop by. On Saturday and Sunday afternoons, local musicians claim the porch; the interior showcases the work of area artists.

Kulinski honed her culinary expertise at the Occidental Arts & Ecology Center, an educational retreat center, eco–think tank, and home to Mother Garden, one of California's first certified organic farms. OAEC's kitchen is charged with preparing meals for steadily arriving retreat and study groups. In her two years of cooking there, Kulinski occasionally helped out friends in need of a hand with their catering or restaurant businesses. One of those friends was Café Aquatica's longtime owner. "I not only loved his café," Kulinski says, "I also loved being on the coast." When the owner suggested in 2018 that she buy the place, it was a done deal.

> **"I like to say that the café is solar powered. When the sun is out, we're busy." –Chef-owner Rachel Kulinski**

Top left: *Granola made from scratch. Photo courtesy Café Aquatica/Giant Eye Photography*

Above left: *Musicians play on the porch on weekends. Photo courtesy Café Aquatica/Nicole Caliva Photography*

Top center: *Pour-over coffee is a specialty. Photo courtesy Café Aquatica/Giant Eye Photography*

Top right: *Rachel preparing pour-over coffee. Photo courtesy Café Aquatica/Giant Eye Photography*

Above right: *Café Aquatica idyllically positioned at the mouth of the Russian River. Photo courtesy Travel Agent Apparel/Maria*

Kulinski made a few changes—enlarging the deck and covering it for sheltered seating on non-fair-weather days, and extensively refining the menu to reflect her personal taste and customer suggestions. While acknowledging that the restaurant business is challenging, she quickly adds, "When you love what you do and follow your passion, you'll never work a day in your life."

10439 Hwy. 1, Jenner, 707-865-2251
cafeaquaticajenner.com

THE MATHESON

Choose your dining experience

There's lots going on at Dustin Valette's 15,700-square-foot, three-story dining experience on the edge of Healdsburg's Plaza. The ground floor houses the Matheson, Valette's high-end, farm-focused restaurant. Seating is at redwood tables hand-hewed by Andrew Somawang, a Sebastopol wood sculptor and guitar maker. Murals by local artist Jay Mercado celebrate the county's agricultural heritage. Look up: the ceiling mimics a wine barrel. The host stand at the entry is an old Italian wine barrel that once held E. & J. Gallo wines.

You can reserve a spot at the chef's counter, if you're lucky, to watch Valette and his team in action. There is also a 12-seat sushi counter offering a front-row view of nigiri stunners under creation. In addition to a well-stocked wine cellar, a space-age wall dispenses 88 wines on tap. A bar whips up craft cocktails.

A different dining experience awaits upstairs at the Matheson's casual sibling. Take the staircase or elevator to Roof 106, named for the restaurant's street address. A wood-fired oven centers bustling indoor-outdoor spaces overlooking leafy Healdsburg below. Order a specialty cocktail or a glass of wine; the menu lists pizzas and such. Unlike the Matheson's reservations-only policy, service is first-come, first-served.

Valette began his culinary journey at age 13 washing dishes at Catelli's in Geyserville. After graduating from the Culinary Institute of America, he continued to hone his expertise in the kitchens of some of the West Coast's most celebrated restaurants. In 2015, he opened Valette in downtown Healdsburg, showcasing the bounty of his Sonoma County roots in a space that once held the 1940s bakery of his great-grandfather, Honoré Valette. It was the second bakery

Top left: *Flat bread receives dollops of caviar. Photo courtesy Sonoma County Tourism*

Above left: *Sushi nigri from the sushi bar. Photo courtesy Michael B. Woolsey*

Top right: *Dustin Valette, The Matheson owner/chef. Photo courtesy Sonoma County Tourism*

Above right: *Exterior as seen through the trees on shady Matheson Street. Photo courtesy Michael B. Woolsey*

for the French immigrant. In the 1920s, steps away from the plaza, Honoré operated his Snowflake Bakery. Dustin watched as the site remained vacant for years; when it finally went up for sale, fearful for what might become of the historic building, he bought it. After years of planning and construction, the Matheson welcomed its first diners in the fall of 2021.

106 Matheson St., Healdsburg, 707-723-1106
themathESON.com

Chef Valette can be seen at Healdsburg farmers market pulling along his classic Radio Flyer wagon piled with menu inspirations.

JOURNEYMAN MEAT CO

A family tradition

Peter Seghesio was but three years old when his father began to teach him sausage making. The curing of meat, after all, was a family tradition, one that Pete's great-grandparents, Edoardo and Angela Seghesio, had brought with them from Italy in 1895. In that same year, they planted a small vineyard, the first of what was to become Seghesio Family Vineyards. Meat curing and sausage making continued as a family tradition through the years—as it did with many of the area's multi-generational Italian families—with Pete graduating from tying sausage into links as a three-year-old to raising hogs destined to be turned into a variety of cured meats. Until 2011, generations of Seghesios gathered with friends for annual wine-fueled sausage-making parties; 2011 was the year that Seghesio Family Vineyards was sold to the Crimson Wine Group.

Pete had served as CEO of Seghesio Family Vineyards for 25 years, and with the sale he was left feeling at loose ends. Increasingly his thoughts turned to the family's tradition. Wanting to learn more, he followed his family's roots, traveling to Italy to learn the Italian style of whole animal butchery and the art of handcrafted, cured meats with masters of the craft. Journeyman Meat Co. was born.

Other meats, such as aged cuts of estate-raised beef and heritage breed pork, are displayed in the shop's cold case. Salumi,

Gundlach Bundschu, in the Sonoma Valley, is by far the oldest family-owned winery in the county; it was established in 1858. Until it was sold, Seghesio was the second oldest, leaving that honor to Foppiano Vineyards, which was established in 1896.

Top left: *Pete's father, Eugene, pictured among Seghesio winery's gigantic redwood tanks.*

Above left: *Peter and Cathy Seghesio*

Top center: *Sausage making, a Seghesio family tradition*

Middle center: *Meat slicer precisely at work*

Top right: *Peter Seghesio, wearing his "Pete Eats Meat" apron, hoisted aloft in a Panzano, Italy butcher shop.*

Above right: *Journeyman products. All photos courtesy Journeyman Meat Co.*

however, is the star, made from recipes painstakingly tested, created with patience, and assembled from the best of local ingredients.

Carry a selection home or grab a seat at an indoor or outdoor table, ordering from a menu that includes sandwiches, pizzas, and—not to be passed up—an artisanal salumi board. Bites of cheese, olives, and perhaps pickled vegetables come with it. The perfect accompaniment? A glass of hearty zinfandel from a Seghesio vineyard.

404 Center St., Healdsburg, 707-395-6328
journeymanmeat.com

CATELLI'S

Third-generation Italian

Catelli's has a long history in Geyserville, population around 1,000. Santi and Virginia Catelli opened their restaurant in 1936, hanging a sign over the door that identified it as the Rex. The Catellis would have preferred that the eatery carry their name, but money was tight and the local sign maker had one on hand that a customer had failed to pick up. Dining was unpretentious Italian fare; Santi and Virginia and their two sons, Richard and Nello, lived upstairs.

When he was in his 20s, Richard was enjoying the big city life of Chicago when his parents asked him to return home and help run the restaurant. That was in the 1960s. Reluctantly he returned to Geyserville. A few years later, as owner-operator, he ordered a new sign: "Catelli's The Rex."

Today a third generation of Catellis, siblings Domenica and Nicholas, operate the restaurant in its familiar spot—"The Rex" long ago abandoned from signage that now simply reads "Catelli's." Nicholas runs the front of the house, and Domenica is the executive chef.

Domenica brought with her an impressive resume as both chef and media personality, serving as a recurring judge on *Iron Chef America* and working behind the scenes at the Food Network and with celebrity chefs on *Oprah* and the *Today Show*. When Stefani Joanne Angelina Germanotta—better known as Lady Gaga—stopped by Catelli's, it was because Domenica was a consultant for the singer's parents' homestyle Italian eatery, Joanne Trattoria, on Manhattan's Upper West Side.Today she happily oversees the classic Italian-American dishes Catelli's has long been known

Left: *Catelli's street view. Photo courtesy Sonoma County Tourism*

Top center: *Signature ravioli. Photo courtesy Sonoma County Tourism*

Above center: *Interior, 1997. Photo courtesy Catelli's*

Top right: *Nicholas and Domenica, third-generation owners. Photo courtesy Catelli's*

Above right: *Interior today. Photo courtesy Catelli's*

for while incorporating ingredients from local organic farmers. Original items are paired with bright new creations such as "The Pasta of the Moment." Domenica's take on her grandmother's lasagna is always on the menu—10 paper-thin layers of hand-made pasta, organic tomato sauce, and ricotta-and-herb filling. It manages to be both surprisingly light and hearty at the same time.

21047 Geyserville Ave., Geyserville, 707-857-3471
mycatellis.com

Geyserville earned its name due to its proximity to geothermal springs in the Mayacamas Mountains that became tourist attractions in the mid-1800s. The town retains the ambiance of the era with wooden boardwalks and centuries-old storefronts.

PARISH CAFÉ

New Orleans through and through

Rob Lippincott grew up in New Orleans dreaming of becoming a professional fisherman, a dream not quite as envisioned when he took a job as a charter skipper. While taking others out to fish, he began to attract attention as a darn good cook. Cooking had been Lippincott's fallback job since his first venture into a professional kitchen at a New Orleans po'boy shack as a teenager.

Then he met his wife, Karla, whose family owns Costeaux French Bakery in Healdsburg. Looking around the wine-country town far from New Orleans, he wondered, "How might I fit in?" Together they came up with the answer: a café serving the food he knew best—authentic Cajun and Creole New Orleans fare.

An 1890s house in need of loving care became available not far from Healdsburg's central plaza. In 2012, the Lippincotts opened Parish Café with a breakfast and lunch menu offering such New Orleans comfort-food standbys as pain perdu, shrimp and grits, and of course po'boys. Customers lined up for freshly made beignets available throughout the day.

The Parish Café was successful, but the wildfires that Sonoma County endured in 2019 and 2020 took their toll on the Lippincott family. After facing three evacuations and feeling reluctant to face the possibility of another, they decided to head back south.

Waiting in the wings were the perfect buyers, Healdsburg second-home owners Gareth and Lynette Owens. "When we were in town, the Parish was our 'go-to' for breakfast," Lynette says.

"You can put your Californication on everything, but don't mess with my food." –Rob Lippincott

Top left: *Sign assures Beignets All Day. Photo courtesy Yvonne Horn*

Above left: *Beignets, New Orleans's special treat. Photo courtesy Parish Café*

Top right: *Shrimp and grits. Photo courtesy Parish Café*

Above right: *Parish Café, New Orleans in Healdsburg. Photo courtesy John Storey*

Gareth brought years of restaurant experience to the venture. "I've worked in and around the industry ever since my mom let me," he says. In 2021, they bought the Parish Café lock, stock, and recipes and moved their family full time to Healdsburg. Without missing a beat, the Parish Café continues to offer Rob's New Orleans comfort food, beignets throughout the day included.

60 Mill St., Healdsburg, 707-431-8474
theparishcafe.com

PICK'S DRIVE-IN

Still a refresher

Claudia Clow was Pick's Drive-In's fourth owner when she bought the white and green roadside burger shack on the south end of town in 1990. She was also working as a dispatcher for the Cloverdale Police Department, answering the station phones from 5:30 p.m. to 9 p.m. after working the grill until 3:30. When she found herself answering the phone with "Hello, Pick's," she knew that one or the other had to go. It was the police department.

Clow's purchase was a beloved town landmark that had opened in 1923 as a Reed & Bell Root Beer "refreshery." Today it is one of the oldest hamburger joints in America.

In 1950, Mayo and Johnnie Pickard bought the refresher, bringing with them the secret red relish recipe they'd used on their hamburgers at the café they'd operated in Santa Rosa's Greyhound bus station. Painting over the orange and black Reed & Bell sign, they renamed the place Pick's.

Through the decades of Clow's ownership, the looks of the place and the menu changed remarkably little; the hamburgers continued to make use of the famous red relish, cooked up six gallons at a time. A 1920s-era cash register accepted purchases. The original Reed & Bell sign found a place under the menu board, layers of paint removed by a customer to reveal the pre-Pickard signage.

Longtime customers continued to drop by to reminisce about when car hops delivered trays of food. Regulars arrived to place their usual order, kids hopped off their bicycles for an ice cream cone, and travelers on their way to the coast pulled in for a bite and a break—Pick's as it had always been and continues to be.

Top left: *Street sign. Photo courtesy Sonoma County Tourism*

Above left: *Original Reed & Bell sign. Photo courtesy Yvonne Horn*

Top right: *Little changed since 1923. Photo courtesy Chowhound*

Above right: *Best burger in town, ready to go. Photo courtesy Sonoma County Tourism*

In 2016, David Alioto, who'd revamped a former A&W into Healdsburg's popular Healdsburger, purchased Pick's, vowing to keep its 1923 charm and its secret red relish recipe intact. Stop by to see if that is so.

117 S Cloverdale Blvd., Cloverdale, 707-894-2962
healdsburger.com

FEED SONOMA

Mahalo FEEDbins

"FEED," an acronym for Farmers Exchange of Earthly Delights, began in 2011 as a walk-in cooler in Tim Page's garage. Page, after 10 years of working as an institutional stockbroker, had the area's independent farmers on his mind—the uphill battle small ranchers and growers face in a food system that favors big agriculture. He began to cultivate a network of wholesale buyers in the North Bay—grocery stores, restaurants, corporate kitchens, and caterers—with the idea of putting together a varied, resilient, reliable product distribution channel.

Page's end goal for FEED Sonoma was that it become a cooperative, but first it had to prove itself to the independent farming community as a viable, dependable enterprise. In 2020, with infrastructure firmly in place, FEED Sonoma became California's first fresh-food employee- and farmer-owned cooperative. Then the pandemic hit, and FEED's wholesale network disintegrated.

With farmers and ranchers holding on by their fingernails, FEED quickly transitioned to delivering multi-farm FEEDbins directly to consumers. Hundreds of subscribers signed up for a weekly box of organically and sustainably grown produce harvested by some 50-plus independent growers. Bins accounted for 75 percent

The Hawaiian words for welcome and thanks, and used to describe the FEEDbins' sizes, *ohana* and *keiki*, pay tribute to Tim Page's years of inspirational living on Maui, where he learned the native language and tenets of their culture from Hawaiian elders.

Top left: *Longer Table Farm, FEED Sonoma producer. Photo courtesy FEED Sonoma/ Paige Green*

Above left: *FEEDbin content. Photo courtesy FEED Sonoma*

Top right: *Tim Page. Photo courtesy FEED Sonoma*

Above right: *Freckle Farm, FEED Sonoma producer. Photo courtesy FEED Sonoma/ Paige Green*

of the cooperative's revenue during the pandemic and continue as an important component today.

Bins come in two sizes. Ohana bins are filled with as many as 11 seasonal items—leafy greens, a variety of vegetables, and fruits. Keiki boxes contain two or three items fewer. Bins are dropped off at hubs for subscriber pick-up or home delivered for an added charge. Subscriptions are available for a weekly or bi-weekly bin, or for a single box as needed. Advance notice lets subscribers know what the upcoming week's bin of fresh-from-the-farm products will hold.

5400 Old Redwood Hwy. N, Petaluma, 707-508-7702
feedsonoma.com

DIAVOLA PIZZERIA

Rethinking pizzas

In a 2016 story for the *Santa Rosa Press Democrat*, feature writer Diane Peterson wrote about Santi, an Italian restaurant in tiny Geyserville. For a half-dozen years until it closed in 2008, Santi was the "Chez Panisse" of Sonoma County, an a la Alice Waters incubator of young chefs embracing the freshest and best. As Peterson wrote, "The eager young chefs met each labor-intensive challenge with enthusiasm. Pasta made from scratch? No problem. Homemade breadsticks? Sure! Kitchen garden? Why not." The team wore T-shirts printed with their motto, "Setting Italian cooking back 75 years."

Dino Bugica was one of that team. Although he was born in Reno, his family roots run deep in Tuscany—roots that led him to cook his way around Italy for a good many years. Shortly after Santi opened, Dino and his Italian wife, Sonja, dined at the Geyserville eatery. Impressed, he quit his chef position in Hawaii and joined Santi's team as pasta chef and instigator of house-cured salumi.

When Santi closed, the young chefs moved on to establish restaurants of their own elsewhere. With one exception. Bugica stayed in Geyserville, opening Diavola up the street in a 1900s–era building that was once the Odd Fellows Hall.

He calls the cookery at his devilishly good Diavola *cucina povera*, "food of the poor," the time-honored tradition of making the most of whatever ingredients are at hand. Poor you would happily be tucking into any of Bugica's wood-fired Neapolitan pizzas, some of which introduce unexpected ingredients; recently Kewpie, a Japanese mayonnaise, found its way onto the Dictator pizza. Pastas and meat dishes also receive unusual twists; an

Left: *Diavola sign hangs out front of what was once Geyserville's Odd Fellows Hall*

Center: *Diavola chef, Dino Bugica*

Top right: *Diavola sign hangs out front of what was once Geyserville's Odd Fellows Hall*

Above right: *Pizza slides out of Diavola's wood-fired oven. All photos courtesy Sonoma County Tourism*

antipasto of salumi, house-cured in the time-honored way, is not to be missed.

Pizzas, however, are Diavola's star—as many as 16 offered on any given day—with Bugica continuing to raise the bar on what has been around the Mediterranean for some 2,000 years.

21021 Geyserville Ave., Geyserville, 707-814-0111
diavolapizzeria.com

"Looking forward while honoring the past was a recurring theme at Santi, which quickly gained a reputation for serving old-school Italian dishes utilizing new-school ingredients."
–Diane Peterson, *Santa Rosa Press Democrat*

DEPOT HOTEL

An eatery since 1890

The Depot Hotel was built as a family home in 1870 from stone cut and carried from General Mariano Vallejo's quarries. Later, new owner Giacomo Mazza, an Italian stonemason, repurposed its living room into a saloon. When the Northern Pacific Railway extended its service into the town of Sonoma in 1890, new tracks were laid alongside Mazza House, and the depot was built across the street. To serve arriving passengers, the railroad bought the property and opened it as the Depot Hotel.

The historic stone building on First Street began its longest period of sole ownership in 1985, when the Ghilarduccis came to town. That would be Virginia "Gia" and Michael Ghilarducci, who bought the Depot Hotel to create a restaurant downstairs and raise their three children above.

Gia and Michael, who had known each other since high school in San Francisco, came to Sonoma with big culinary ideas. Michael, a graduate of San Francisco City College's hotel and restaurant program, had already managed three Bay Area restaurants. In short order, Michael was in the Depot Hotel kitchen turning out noteworthy, rustic Tuscan dishes. Soon after, the couple's Depot Hotel Cooking School was deemed a success; the duo led culinary cruises and co-taught with Jacques Pépin in France. In time, wines from the Ghilarduccis' Lake County vineyard and winery were added to the restaurant's list; a garden courtyard, complete with a reflection pond, was added for special events.

In 2014, Michael died. Son Antonio "Tony," with his cooking craft honed at such notable eateries as the French Laundry, took over as executive chef.

Eight years later, Gia announced with mixed feelings that, after 50 years in the business, it was time to retire. Tony, too,

Top left: *Hotel street view. Photo courtesy Yvonne Horn*

Above left: *Rustic Italian fare from the Depot Hotel's kitchen. Photo courtesy Depot Hotel*

Top right: *Photo courtesy Depot Hotel*

Above right: *Gia and Michael Ghilarducci. Photo courtesy Depot Hotel*

expressed a desire to move on. Ken and Stacy Mattson, operating as Sonoma's Best Hospitality Group, quickly stepped up to become the Depot Hotel's new owners. In saying goodbye, Gia relayed to the staff the Mattsons' assurance that nothing would change. Depot Hotel's loyal diners took a deep breath and hoped that would be so.

241 First St. W, Sonoma, 707-938-2980
depotsonoma.com

The Northern Pacific Railway tracks that ran through Sonoma are now a rail-to-trail path much used by bicyclists and walkers.

BREWSTERS BEER GARDEN

Down by the river

You could easily pass 350-seat Brewsters on Petaluma's main drag north of Washington Street without an inkling it was there. Pause a moment to admire a garden of water-wise succulents and native grasses that turns out to be—wait a minute—a living roof covering the Brewsters's kitchen. To find the entrance, take the adjacent alley downhill to a dead-end stretch of Water Street. Co-owners Mike Goebel and Chris Beerman planned it so that Brewsters would face the Petaluma River.

Although Brewsters is hidden away in plain sight, since 2016, Petaluma has embraced the camaraderie of a Munich-style beer garden in Northern California. The family-friendly, dog-friendly eatery has craft beers, an appealing pub-grub menu, and live music on a stage near the firepit.

Beerman, a North Carolinian, has worked in restaurants since his teenage days; his grandfather owned fried chicken eateries. After studying culinary arts in Rhode Island, he sharpened his skills in Colorado restaurants before moving to San Francisco, where he established his successful Citizen's Band restaurant. Goebel grew up in Centralia, Washington, and attended San Francisco State on a soccer scholarship enhanced with bartending gigs. After graduating, he opened several bars, among them the popular Bloodhound located across the street from Citizen's

Brewsters isn't so named because of its brews. Researching old city maps, Goebel and Beerman discovered that the area was entered as Brewsters Addition.

Top left: *Bar seating. Photo courtesy Brewsters Beer Garden*

Above left: *Pub-grub mac 'n cheese. Photo courtesy Brewsters Beer Garden*

Above center: *Family- and dog-friendly atmosphere. Photo courtesy Brewsters Beer Garden*

Top right: *Brewsters's Water Street entrance. Photo courtesy MAD Architecture*

Above right: *Hamburgers, messy to eat but delicious. Photo courtesy Brewsters Beer Garden*

Band. The two owners became close friends and began playing around with the idea of a joint venture. Brewsters Beer Garden was on its way.

Wood-fired smokers and grills on the patio offer the clue that barbeque is big at Brewsters; lucky you if you're there while a whole, butterflied hog is wrangled onto the grill. Servers endlessly deliver messy-to-eat burgers with a big pile of perfect fries alongside, but you're also likely to find mac and cheese, buttermilk fried chicken, and Texas-style brisket on the changing daily menu.

Sunny Saturdays can become raucous and busy, but Brewsters is a family joint; rest assured that things never get Viking-level crazy.

229 Water St. N, Petaluma, 707-981-8330
brewstersbeergarden.com

LIBERTY DUCKS

A quacking-good duck

Jim Reichardt always had a pet duck. When he was a kid, one rode around with him on his bicycle and later, bundled up in a blanket, accompanied him in his convertible. "Ducks bond fast and make great pets," he says.

That aside, they also make great eating, as the Reichardt family has known for more than 125 years. Otto Reichardt founded Reichardt Duck Farm in San Francisco in 1901, raising White Pekin ducks, a variety developed by the Chinese from the wild mallard. (Those luscious, lacquer-skinned ducks hanging in Chinese meat markets and served as Peking duck in restaurants are White Pekins.) A fourth and fifth generation of Reichardts continue to raise the variety on their Reichardt Duck Farm in Petaluma, with some 40,000 ducks harvested each week.

Jim's father, John, encouraged his children not to put all their ducks in one coop, so to speak, and not feel obligated to enter the family business. After college, Jim worked for a number of years as an architectural photographer before returning to the family farm in 1982.

Ten years later, he struck out on his own, founding Sonoma County Poultry in answer to high-end restaurant chefs asking for a larger, meatier, leaner, and more flavorful duck. A strain of Pekin duck developed in Denmark fulfilled the chefs' wishes, and Sonoma

Liberty Ducks's website lists its North Bay grocery partners and the San Francisco and North Bay restaurants that feature Liberty Ducks on their menus. Home cooks will find recipes on the website, including one from Martha Stewart.

Top left: *Liberty Ducks raised in an open environment. Photo courtesy Cream Meat Co.*

Above left: *Duck legs, cooked to juicy perfection. Photo courtesy Liberty Ducks*

Top right: *Jim Reichardt. Photo courtesy Liberty Ducks*

Above right: *Duck sausages. Photo courtesy Liberty Ducks*

County possessed the climate required to raise them. "Liberty Ducks" struck Jim as a suitable name for the ducks he raises in an open environment, on straw litter. The ducks are fed a diet of corn and grain with no added antibiotics or hormones. "The best, most flavorful duck raised in the country today," Jim says of his Liberty Ducks. Chef accolades agree.

707-791-0397
libertyducks.com

BARNDIVA

A family affair

"It's our heartbeat," Barndiva owners Jil and Geoffrey Hales say of the Anderson Valley farm where the family has organically dry-farmed apples, figs, chestnuts, and more for four generations. It's no wonder that the architecture of the Healdsburg restaurant they opened in 2006 is that of a barn—a barn with a diva kitchen regarded by Michelin in 2021 as star worthy when overseen by chef Jordan Rosas.

Although it looks as if it has been there forever, the barn, with its high-ceilinged interior and lofty windows, was built from scratch. Tables are hewn from Indonesian mahogany and embossed with the barn in silhouette. Farm-animal-inspired wire sculptures create shadowy images on the walls. Large floral arrangements from plants grown on the Anderson Valley farm grace the dining and bar areas; farm-grown herbs and edible flowers embellish the plates emerging from the kitchen. The overall effect is elegant yet welcomingly comfortable.

Each member of the Hales family has a role to play. Jil is Barndiva's creative director, while Geoffrey is chief financial officer. Jil also oversees the restaurant's creative cocktail program with daughter Isabel; the two also produce "Eat the View," Barndiva's peek behind the kitchen door and at goings-on at the Anderson Valley farm. Son Lukka is the driving force behind the restaurant's wide range of hospitality and wine programs.

As for the current kitchen team, Erik Anderson replaced Rosas as executive chef in January 2022, bringing with him a lengthy resume that included stints at the French Laundry and three-Michelin-star Noma in Copenhagen, named "best restaurant in the world" in 2021. Neidy Venegas, pastry chef, continues to win applause for her stunningly intricate and creative dining finales.

Top left: *Chef Jordan Rosas. Photo courtesy Barndiva*

Above left: *Restaurant built to look as if it had been there forever. Photo courtesy Barndiva*

Top right: *Barndiva team celebrates Michelin star. Photo courtesy Barndiva*

Above right: *Edible flowers decorate plates. Photo courtesy Sonoma County Tourism*

While both the family and the entire Barndiva team were effervescently happy in 2021 to receive a Michelin star, the Hales could not help but exclaim, ". . . after 17 years!"

231 Center St., Healdsburg, 707-431-0100
barndiva.com

"No matter how delicious the dish, beautiful the room, extraordinary the floral arrangements, or seductive the lighting, genuine hospitality is what the guest remembers the most."
–the Hales family

GEYSERVILLE GUN CLUB

Seasonal craft cocktails meet history

In a gun club, who'd expect to see a large poster of Sophia Loren, sad-eyed and legs akimbo, as she was in the 1955 Italian film *Woman of the River*, or a restroom with bubblegum-pink potties and matching sink? Well, a mule deer trophy does gaze down at the goings-on in that pink restroom. Chef Dino Bugica, who opened the watering hole adjacent to his Diavola, explains the deer head as an example of his dedication to whole-animal butchery. The pink bathroom fixtures? He likes pink. As for Sophia Loren, she's his ideal of a beautiful woman.

There's not a gun in sight, so why the name? Run across the street to Bosworth & Son General Merchandise—the wee hamlet's community hub since 1911—and the current Bosworth will tell you that during World War II, the all-volunteer California State Guard put steel plates in the basement of the Odd Fellows Hall and turned it into a practice range for .22 rifles and pistols. The gun racks, still present in the basement, inspired Bugica to pay tribute to a piece of Geyserville history.

Adam Welch, who'd been shaking up wine country's cocktail scene for at least a dozen years, launched the bar program. On the drinks menu, expect cheekily named seasonal cocktails, standard mixed drinks, wines, and local beers on tap. Bar food, although emerging from a conjoined kitchen, is entirely unlike neighboring Diavola's rustic Italian fare. Bugica describes it as small portions

"Chef-driven bar bites, irreverence, and absurdity on tap."
–Heather Irwin, *Santa Rosa Press Democrat* dining editor

Top left: *Adam Welch shakes it up. Photo courtesy Geyserville Gun Club*

Above left: *Craft cocktails a specialty. Photo courtesy Visit Geyserville*

Top right: *Unique eats emerge from the kitchen. Photo courtesy Visit Geyserville*

Above right: *Historic Odd Fellows Hall. Photo courtesy Visit Geyserville*

with Japanese, Chinese, and Southeast Asian flavors. Think such dishes as pickled duck eggs, fall-off-the-bones Korean short ribs, and lumpia stuffed with sausage and shrimp.

On weekends, when live bands are booked, tables are pushed aside to make room for dancing. The moose-antler chandelier (glass, not real moose) hanging near the entrance rocks. Sophia Loren looks on, trying her best not to smile and tap her foot.

21025 Geyserville Ave., Geyserville, 707-814-0036
geyservillegunclub.com

HARVEY'S DONUTS

Mini madness

Dollops of dough pop through a funnel into a stream of sizzling oil. Flippers turn them side to side until they emerge cooked to perfection—tender interior, crispy exterior. Twelve bite-sized cake donuts, finished off with a dozen or more options, from powdered sugar to an assortment of glazes, are handed across the counter in a colorful paper cone.

Harvey Cohen's machine can turn out 1,200 donuts an hour. "The longest you'll have to wait," he says, "is however long it takes you to decide on how you want it finished."

Fifteen years ago, Cohen was at an art fair selling vintage seed packets dating from a time when seed envelopes featured original art. Sources of his supply were dwindling because most gardeners, then as now, tossed the packets when the last seed hit the dirt. A thought popped into his head—a good forever business would be selling an item as beloved as, say, hot dogs. With that, he remembered a prototype of a tabletop donut machine he'd seen demonstrated at a trade show some 20 years before. Cohen tracked the engineer down and bought it.

He started off at farmers markets, ponytail and mustache topped off with his now trademark stovepipe hat, wife Georgia by his side. Lines formed.

The corporate world began calling, with Cohen booking 15 to 20 gigs a month, some with 1,000-plus attendees. He tracked down more vintage machines. Today he has nine machines, a fleet of five vans, and 15 employees—including his two daughters, who've joined the enterprise.

In the town of Sonoma, his mini-donut machines operate in two venues. The first is on Railroad Avenue, a family-friendly venue

Top left: *Donuts with a selection of toppings. Photo Harvey's Donuts.*

Above left: *Harvey Cohen in his trademark hat works the machine. Photo Harvey's Donuts*

Top right: *Harvey's Donuts sign, El Paseo Sonoma Plaza location. Photo courtesy Yvonne Horn*

Above right: *Donuts ready for eating. Photo courtesy Harvey's Donuts*

beloved by locals for such events as birthday parties. Recently opened is his tiny shop in the El Paseo courtyard, steps away from the tourist-packed plaza.

Cohen recounts many memorable tiny-donut-making moments. Among them, a young couple stopped by. When their order was ready, the young man dropped to one knee, slipped a donut on the woman's finger, and asked, "Will you marry me?"

414 First St. E, Sonoma
707-246-5928

9030 Railroad Ave., Sonoma
707-935-5908

harveysdonuts.com

Harvey Cohen's recipe for success: "Be in the right place at the right time and see possibilities others don't."

CAFÉ LA HAYE

Strumming happily along

"Serve breakfast; everyone will come." That was the advice in 1996 when partners John McReynolds and Saul Gropman opened Café La Haye in Sonoma's century-old La Haye building. "Everyone" didn't come. Breakfast was a bust, but dinner turned out to be a winner. Michael Bauer, then the dining critic for the *San Francisco Chronicle*, gave the café rave reviews and listed La Haye for 15 years in a row on his list of top 100 Bay Area restaurants.

After 10 years, McReynolds moved on to become culinary director at Stone Edge Farm. Gropman became the café's sole proprietor. This begs the question: How does an accomplished classical guitarist end up owning one of Sonoma's most beloved restaurants?

It began with a teenaged Gropman washing dishes at a neighborhood restaurant to pay for a guitar to play Beatles songs. This segued into classical guitar at the Manhattan School of Music that, in turn, led to teaching at San Francisco State University. Despite teaching and performing, Gropman found time to be actively engaged in San Francisco's restaurant scene, notably as manager of the estimable South Park Café and as partner in the Italian eatery Ecco, both now closed.

As it enters its third decade, dining at Café La Haye remains a fresh experience, with large contemporary paintings on the walls, an airy high-peaked ceiling, and two-level seating that makes it possible for everyone to see and be seen. There are 34 diners when the small space is full. Gropman still graciously greets and seats guests. Add to that an ever-changing menu created by chef Jeffrey Lloyd, who entered the kitchen in 2009 with a resume that included the Culinary Institute of America in Hyde Park and executive chef at Las Vegas's Bellagio.

Top left: *Lamb chops from Chef Lloyd's tiny kitchen. Photo courtesy Sonoma County Tourism*

Above left: *Chef Jeffrey Lloyd. Photo Sonoma Valley Visitors Bureau*

Top right: *Café's interior, seating on two levels. Photo courtesy Sonoma County Tourism*

Center right: *Saul Gropman, Café La Haye's owner/host. Photo courtesy Sonoma Valley Tourist Bureau*

Above right: *Café earns its name from its location in historic La Haye building. Photo courtesy Sonoma Valley Visitors Bureau*

Arguably the best seats in the house are at the four-seat counter, where one can watch Lloyd in his broom-closet-sized kitchen turning out dishes that continue to make the Michelin Bib Gourmand stand up and take notice.

140 E Napa St., Sonoma, 707-935-5994
cafelahaye.com

TILTED SHED CIDERWORKS

Apples and time

The shed on their farm is so decrepit that Scott Heath and his wife, Ellen Cavalli, wonder daily how it remains standing. They also look on it as a good omen: if the shed can hold its own, so should their cidery in vineyard-obsessed Sonoma County. Since launching their ciderworks in the spring of 2011, so far so good. Better than good.

Heath and Cavalli describe their ciderworks as "an idea gone wild" when the two were trying their hand at organic farming in Northern New Mexico. A gnarled, old apple orchard claimed a chunk of their small piece of land. Heath, who according to Cavalli is a bit of a mad scientist, began to wonder whether the orchard's Jonathan, Golden Delicious, and Red Delicious apples might add up to a good quaff. Cavalli lobbed apples into a barrel press, Heath did the cranking, and the barn did the rest, taking over the juice's care during months of fermentation. The result surprised them both. Study, research, and trial and error followed before they took the leap into creating a bona fide ciderworks. What better place to establish their venture than the historic apple-growing hills of Sonoma's west county?

More than a dozen years later, a two-acre orchard planted with traditional cider apple and perry pear varieties produces the basic ingredients for Tilted Shed ciders, amplified by fruit from organic growers located within 35 miles of the cidery. No bulk juice, concentrate, colorings, or flavorings are used—just apples, unrefined, unfiltered, and wild fermented.

Tilted Shed's ciders are available for tasting in Windsor's Artisan Alley, a collection of small producers of cider, wine, and spirits. During tasting hours, big doors roll up along the colorful

Left: *Tilted Shed Graviva celebrates the Gravenstein apple. Photo courtesy Sonoma County Farm Trails*

Top center: *Tilted Shed ciders ready for tasting. Photo courtesy Sonoma County Tourism*

Above center: *Barreled Wild Graviva, made entirely from Gravenstein apples. Photo courtesy Yvonne Horn*

Right: *Huband and wife cider team, Ellen Cavalli and Scott Heath, with their namesake tilted shed. Photo courtesy Karen Pavone Photography*

alley, revealing production facilities and adjacent tasting bars with umbrella-shaded patio areas set up out front.

Tilted Shed offers tastings, with at least a dozen ciders available by the glass or in flights of five. A flight, when put together with Tilted Shed's expert behind-the-bar guidance, reveals an amazing variety of styles—dry, semi-sweet, méthode champenoise sparkling, and brandy-like for after-dinner sipping.

7761 Bell Rd., Windsor, 707-657-7796
tiltedshed.com

Graviva–pronounced "Gra-VEE-va" as in "Viva la Grav(enstein)!" –pays homage to Sonoma County's rich apple heritage and is Tilted Shed's most crowd-pleasing cider.

ERNIE'S TIN BAR

Talk on tap

Don't expect eats at Ernie's Tin Bar, unless you count all the peanuts you can shell and the bags of chips and such for sale in the bowl on the bar. As for uniqueness, there's plenty to be had. Take the "no cellphone talking" rule. Signage in the parking lot and inside gives fair warning. Those who persist, after a polite request to put their phone away, are asked to leave. Why the policy? Sociability. Patrons are encouraged to talk with one another instead of with someone who isn't there. As might be expected, a good many patron-to-patron conversations begin with talking about no cellphone talking.

For decades, beginning in 1923, the corrugated tin building at the busy intersection of the Lakeville Highway and Stage Gulch Road was an auto and farm equipment repair garage. A 1950s truck with its hood up in the garage part of the bar gives the impression that its owner will be in tomorrow to pick it up. But from its 1920s beginnings, the garage has been more than automotive repair. Sociability is part and parcel of its history. In its earliest days, locals stopped by to exchange the news of the day over a glass of soda water or, with the close of Prohibition, a beer.

Ernie Altenreuther, who carries the name of the original Ernie, shares the Tin Bar's ownership with his cousin Chris Nardone. When they took it over, the choice of beers was limited to the big-name canned eight. A weathered sign out front still advertises ice-cold beer for $1.75, and an icy can of Hamm's can still be had at that price. Walk inside and you'll find the North Bay's largest, most eclectic, and best-curated selection of beers

Top: *Roadside view. Photo courtesy Michael B. Woolsey Photography*

Above left: *Ernie Altenreuther, grandson of original Ernie, tends bar. Photo courtesy Michael B. Woolsey Photography*

Above right: *Chris Nardone pours a pint. Michael B. Woolsey Photography*

and ciders on tap. Who'd expect that if you asked for a suggestion that you might be offered a taste of Mikkeller Spontan Cherry Frederiksdal from Copenhagen?

5100 Lakeville Hwy., Petaluma, 707-762-2075

BELLWETHER FARMS

Cheeses, yogurt, and more

Thirty years ago, when she was in her 50s, Cindy Callahan took a quantum leap from her career as a nurse into something different. Raising lambs into milk-producing sheep was certainly that! Her endeavor was one of the first commercial sheep-milking dairies west of the Mississippi.

The word bellwether has two meanings, both apt for Cindy's farm: "an indicator or predictor of something—the bellwether of change" and "the leading sheep of a flock, with a bell on its neck."

East Friesian sheep, a tall Northern European breed with distinctively longer and more pointed ears, make up Bellwether's flock. Although they produce much less milk than other breeds—averaging less than half a gallon per day—their milk is considered among the richest and has the highest protein content in the world. Ewes bear from one to three lambs a year and sometimes more. You can't take the nurse out of the nurse; to this day, Callahan is on hand for the birth of nearly all the farm's new lambs.

Callahan chose well the land on which to raise her flock. It is located in rolling hills not far from the sea, and fogs and ocean-cooled breezes roll in. This is dairy country; heat stress adversely affects milk production and quality.

The farm became a family endeavor when Cindy's son, Liam Callahan, set aside his UC–Berkeley degree to respond to his mother's suggestion that he learn more about turning sheep's milk into cheese. They spent time in Europe, absorbing traditional cheese-making methods. When Liam married, wife Diana Callahan joined the team, learning the business in the cheese room before moving on to manage the office. Liam now oversees Bellwether Farms's cheese production.

Five different kinds of fresh sheep cheeses, along with two aged, raw cheeses and a ricotta, are made. Sheep's milk yogurt is produced

Top left: *Liam Callahan, left, with wife Diana*

Above left: *Callahan family, Cindy seated with grandchildren, and Diana and Liam*

Above center: *East Friesian sheep, known for milk production*

Top right: *Sheep milk yogurt in a variety of flavors*

Above right: *Cindy Callahan, Bellwether founder. All photos courtesy Bellwether Farms*

both plain and flavored with straight-from-the-orchard organic fruit. Cow's milk cheeses, including ricotta, crème fraiche, and fromage blanc, are made with milk provided by a nearby dairy's Jersey cows. Jerseys, like East Friesian sheep, are known for quality-over-quantity milk.

Thirty years later, Cindy Callahan's quantum leap is doing extraordinarily well in the fog-cooled air of west Sonoma County.

9999 Valley Ford Rd., Petaluma, 707-763-0993
bellwetherfarms.com

Bellwether Farms products are widely available throughout Sonoma County and beyond. Enter your zip code on the website's product map to find nearby locations.

SCREAMIN' MIMI'S

Yell "yes" to a cone or more

"I scream. You scream. We all scream for ice cream!"—if it's Maraline "Mimi" Olson's ice cream, that is. Viewed from the street, her shop inspires cravings, its façade done up in strawberry trimmed with vanilla, with pistachio awnings shading the windows. Order a cone, and at first lick you'll know why Screamin' Mimi's has been voted Sonoma County's best ice cream every year since its 1995 opening.

It began with Mimi trying to duplicate in her home kitchen the ice cream she enjoyed growing up on the East Coast. One particular mixture incorporating coffee, chocolate chips, cookies, and fudge was so good that her husband, Kurt, encouraged her to create a business plan and open a shop. Mimi's Mud remains Screamin' Mimi's best seller, accounting for nearly a third of the shop's overall sales.

That recipe has a lot of competition, however. Some 200 ice cream and sorbet flavors rotate into a daily selection of a dozen or more available for scooping. All are made in small batches using seasonal and local ingredients. Specialty and seasonal flavors, like the lavender people wait for all year, sell out quickly. "Scarcity whets demand," Mimi says.

Including the ice cream, everything is made in house—hot fudge, caramel sauce, waffle cones, whipped cream, and the dough for the cookies that hold together the "sammies." Mimi and Kurt

"When things are really good, people go out for ice cream. When things are really bad, they go out for ice cream."
–Maraline "Mimi" Olson

Top left: *Choice of flavors and size in a house-made waffle cone*

Above left: *Street view of shop painted in ice cream flavored colors*

Right: *Maraline "Mimi" Olson. All photos courtesy Screamin' Mimi's*

personally make most of the ice cream. "I love ice cream. I love my job," Mimi says.

All flavors are sold by weight, not by the scoop, letting customers get and pay for exactly what they want, not what looks good in a cone or dish. If you are hankering for just a small taste of a sundae and not the big dish, feel free to order a one- or two-ouncer. Packed pints for carrying home are enough to serve four or, as Mimi says, "one person who likes to keep it hidden in the freezer."

6902 Sebastopol Ave., Sebastopol, 707-823-5902
screaminmimisicecream.com

EDGE

Largesse from the farm

On one of his morning walks in 1996, Mac McQuown pondered what to call the five acres he and his wife, Leslie, had just purchased west of the town of Sonoma. Stone Edge Farm, of course, named for the century-old rock wall he was following. Ten years later, Stone Edge Farm encompassed 16 acres with over 100 varieties of vegetables, herbs, and fruits organically and sustainably farmed, along with such "pantry items" as olive oil, eggs, and honey. A five-acre vineyard, the farm's centerpiece, and two additional vineyards in the Mayacamas range were yielding notable Bordeaux-style wines.

In 2008, John McReynolds, founding chef and co-owner of Sonoma's Café La Haye, became Stone Edge Farm's culinary director. With the farm's cornucopia as his larder, McReynolds created meals for visitors, special events, and wine club food gatherings paired with Stone Edge Farm wines. His hefty and pictorial *Stone Edge Farm Estate Vineyards & Winery Cookbook* won the prestigious Julia Child First Book Award from the International Association of Culinary Professionals; it was followed by the *Stone Edge Farm Kitchen Larder Cookbook*. In 2013, Fiorella Burton joined McReynolds as executive chef, bringing inspirations from her Peruvian heritage and training at Le Cordon Bleu in Lima.

When a sweet Victorian house across East Napa Street from Café La Haye became available, the McQuowns bought it and, after a sleek update, opened EDGE, the private dining and culinary home for Stone Edge Farm's wine club. So it remained for five years.

Now the word is out that reservations are available for a weekly prix fixe menu created by Burton in her dual role as

Left: *John McReynolds, Stone Edge Farm's original and longtime culinary director. Photo courtesy Stone Edge Farms*

Left center: *Exquisitely plated dishes emerge from the kitchen. Photo courtesy Stone Edge Farm*

Right center top: *Stone Edge Farm's Victorian culinary home in downtown Sonoma. Photo courtesy Yvonne Horn*

Right center above: *Mac and Leslie McQuown. Photo courtesy Stone Edge Farm*

Right: *Fiorella Burton, Stone Edge Farm culinary director and EDGE executive chef. Photo courtesy Stone Edge Farm*

culinary director and executive chef. Your table is yours for the evening for a dining experience that Carey Sweet, *Santa Rosa Press Democrat* restaurant reviewer, reported as both exceptional and a good value, especially considering the amuses, the intermezzos, and the final gift of a mignardise included with the pairings of the farm's wines throughout.

139 E Napa St., Sonoma, 707-935-6520
edgesonoma.com

"People want to relegate 15 minutes to making dinner. I take a different approach. Open a bottle of wine; talk to your wife while you're cooking. It's not an activity to get through. It's the main event." –John McReynolds

SUPER LA FAVORITA

The Springs' favorite grocery

Just north of the city of Sonoma, a trio of unincorporated communities strung along Highway 12—Agua Caliente, Fetters Hot Springs, and Boyes Hot Springs—are collectively known as the Springs, named for the geothermal resorts that beckoned tourists at the turn of the 20th century. The Golden Gate Bridge was yet to be built; all it took for some 70,000 yearly visitors to reach hot, mineral-laden nirvana was a ferry ride across the bay and an 80-cent train ride.

By mid-century, however, the heyday of "taking the waters" was over, leaving hot-spring communities to slowly languish.

In recent years, a transformation has taken place in what has become a largely Hispanic area. Artist-designer Rico Martin changed the everyday façades of a half-dozen businesses along a stretch of Highway 12 into colorful Latin-inspired celebrations of their ownerships. A multi-million-dollar roadway improvement followed, with long-anticipated sidewalks and lighting installed. Dilapidated buildings were torn down, and new shops and housing emerged, turning the Springs from "left behind" to "hip and trendy."

Super La Favorita owner Alfonso Ulloa didn't sign up for a façade transformation, leaving his products to speak for themselves. Standouts at the grocery store are packed-to-order fresh salsas, guacamole, and ceviches of shrimp or fish. As a carniceria, a butcher case stretches along an entire wall filled with the best Harris Ranch cuts, along with prepared fajita mix, fish fillets breaded for frying, pickled pork skins, and carne asada.

The luxurious Sonoma Mission Inn & Spa is the Springs' sole remaining resort.

Top left: *Jars of canned guavas from Mexico*

Above left: *Colorfully painted façades celebrate Latin business ownership*

Top right: *Street view*

Above right: *Unusual packaged spices fill one wall. All photos courtesy Yvonne Horn*

Produce is brought in daily and includes hard-to-find items like fresh turmeric and garbanzo beans still in their pods. Packaged dried spices of every persuasion are hung on a wall; tortillas include those made by a nearby restaurant, Jalisco of Sonoma. An entire counter is filled with an assortment of dried beans of all sizes and maize begging to be turned into posole. Warm tamales are available, and if you're in need of a piñata for an upcoming party, there's a selection dangling from the ceiling.

17484 Sonoma Hwy., Sonoma, 707-938-9607

MIRACLE PLUM

Delicious things made well

There's lots going on behind this tidy, white 116-year-old building's mustard-colored door. Tucked in between two 21st-century multi-story edifices, a swooping sign pointing toward the door offers a laundry list of items: "produce, cheese, coffee, wares, bread, local, gifts, eggs, jam, teas."

So, exactly what is Miracle Plum? Another sign out front reads "Very Open." Give the mustard-colored door a push and walk into what owners Sallie Miller and Gwen Gunheim describe as "an experience of delicious things made well."

Shelves are stocked with dozens of judiciously selected pantry items you didn't know you needed. Among them is an array of spices chosen for their remarkable flavor, such as Burlap & Barrel's Black Urfa Chili and Cinnamon Verum. One shelf is filled with different kinds of vinegars and "almost vinegars," like those from Sonoma Portworks. House-made products are decided crowd-pleasers: granola, shrubs, pickles, spice blends, and jams. Sign up for the Jam Club to receive a seasonal shipment of two jars of jam.

Miller and Gunheim, both of whom grew up in Santa Rosa, are dedicated home cooks. "Growing up in a place of such abundance helped shape our palates and in turn shaped our shop," says Gunheim. "Everything in the shop are things we personally love."

House-made products are made at the nearby Kitchen, along with grab-and-go lunchtime favorites—salads, soups, and sandwiches—prepared for Miracle Plum pick-up. Carry your lunch back to the office or snag a seat at the counter in the shop or at a table in the alley "courtyard." Bar snacks to pair with late-afternoon wines by the glass also come from the Kitchen; set aside the second Thursday of every month for a Meet the Winemaker evening.

Left: *Wine by the glass. Photo courtesy Yvonne Horn*

Right: *Gwen Gunheim, left, Sallie Miller, right, pose outside Miracle Plum. Photo courtesy Made Local/Paige Green*

Collaboration, not competition, is a Miracle Plum byword. That includes the hosting of entrepreneurial pop-up events. Other events come from the creative minds of the Miracle Plum duo. One is the Cookbook Club. At a gathering every few months, members bring dishes for potluck sharing and food talk from a cookbook decided upon in advance by Miller and Gunheim. A small donation goes to the cookbook author's chosen charity.

208 Davis St., Santa Rosa, 707-708-7986
miracleplum.com

The Miracle Plum is a variety of seedless plum invented by famed early-20th-century Sonoma County horticulturist Luther Burbank.

JOHN ASH & Co

The right place at the right time

On a summer evening in 1980, John Ash was dining at Santa Rosa's fanciest establishment. Accompanying his entree were canned green beans—canned green beans at a time of year when fresh vegetables were in abundance! He describes it as being struck by lightning.

Ash, raised on his grandparents' Colorado ranch, watched his grandmother cook meals for ranch hands—with no recipes—on a wood stove. He thought it was magical. So began what was to become a lifelong passion for cooking. The passion followed him while he was working as a photographer and medical illustrator in San Francisco—with a side interest in food styling—and to Del Monte Foods as head of new product development. As a break from corporate life, Europe's cooking schools beckoned. At a little Burgundy inn, morning market visits determined what would emerge from the kitchen that day.

All this led to his 1980 "struck by lightening" moment: Sonoma County, like Burgundy, was a cornucopia of fresh products. Why weren't restaurants using them?

That same year, Ash opened John Ash & Co. in Santa Rosa's Montgomery Village, dedicated to seasonal, fresh, local products. *Gourmet* magazine and the *New York Times*, among others, took notice, dubbing him "the father of wine country cuisine." "I was in the right place at the right time," he says.

The cozy Front Room bar, adjacent to the restaurant, is known for its happy hour bargains and bar menu.

Top left: *Ivy surrounded restaurant sign. Photo courtesy Yvonne Horn*

Left center: *Chef John Ash. Photo courtesy Go Sonoma*

Above left: *Salmon with risotto and asparagus. Photo courtesy Vintners Inn*

Top right: *Vineyard surrounded covered porch dining. Photo courtesy Vintners Inn*

Above right: *Executive Chef Tom Schmidt on a break from his kitchen. Photo courtesy Vintners Inn*

Eight years later, John Ash & Co. moved to a new building among the vineyards at Vintners Inn. There it remains under Ash's name, even though he left the kitchen in 1994. The behind-the-scenes daily grind of running a restaurant had taken its toll. "I realized that what I really like about cooking is yakking about it," he says.

He has continued to do just that, authoring six cookbooks, fulfilling requests for cooking classes and demonstrations across the country and abroad, and for 35 years co-hosting the *Good Food Hour* on KSRO radio with co-foodie Steve Garner.

Three decades after his departure, Ash's eponymous restaurant remains true to his vision under Thomas Schmidt, executive chef for the past 14 years: fine dining driven by local, seasonal ingredients.

4350 Barnes Rd., Santa Rosa, 707-527-7687
vintnersresort.com/dining/john-ash-co

SRJC CULINARY CAFÉ AND BAKERY

Cooks in training

Table linens are white and crisp, glassware gleams, and cutlery is placed just so. It's lunch time at a fine-dining restaurant, right? One would think so, but the uniformed cooks at work in the kitchen wearing small, white hats are students working their way through a course of study in Santa Rosa Junior College's Culinary Arts program. The tall-toque wearers are their instructors.

It is students who greet you at the door, show you to your table, and take your order. The program offers certification instruction in five demanding eight-week blocks of study: serving, front-of-house skills, baking and pastry, restaurant management, and culinary arts. A full-time faculty is supplemented by adjuncts, local chefs sharing their areas of expertise.

Chef Michael Salinger developed the program from what was called Home Economics in 1994. In his nearly 30 years as head toque, Culinary Arts grew out of its original campus setting into a $20 million brick edifice; teaching progressed from preparing staid classics to exploring vegan and gluten-free options.

Instead of amassing a binder of recipes, students learn via demonstration and hands-on practice of fundamental skills—knife handling, prepping, sauteing, and grilling. Diners understand that cooks-in-training are preparing their lunch, and that along with a tasty meal in a charming setting at an attractive price point bumps happen.

Much of the produce that enters the kitchen is grown at the college's Shone Farm, an essential part of the school's Agriculture and Natural Resources program that encompasses 120 acres of managed forest, 100 acres of pastures, 90 acres of vineyards, 12 acres

Top: *Students at work in the Culinary Café kitchen*

Above left: *Retail bakery case*

Above right: Culinary Arts, housed in its own campus edifice. All photos courtesy SRJC Culinary Arts.

planted with crops, and 4 acres planted with olive and apple trees—all sustainably and organically cared for. Among the wines available for sipping are those vinted at Shone Farm.

Coming or going to the café, don't overlook the bakery's glass cases inside the front door. Stocked with pastries, muffins, cookies, and other hard-to-pass-by goodies, the bakery opens at 8 a.m. for those in need of starting their workday with something sweet and a cup of coffee.

1670 Mendocino Ave., Santa Rosa, 707-522-2796
culinary.santarosa.edu/café-bakery

Be aware that both the bakery and the café run on the college's schedule of semester breaks and holidays.

EYE CANDY CHOCOLATIER

Chocolates with a delicious vision

Two half circles tie together the chocolatier's logo, one facing left toward the word "Eye," the other facing right, creating the "C" for candy. To the casual observer it's a simple yet attractive logo. But ophthalmologists immediately get it—it's something they see when checking for glaucoma.

In her busy ophthalmology practice, Dr. Sonja Schluter sees all too many patients facing serious vision problems, primarily glaucoma. In her off time, she retreats to her "happy place," the creation of chocolate truffles.

For years, Schluter's chocolates were made in her home kitchen, becoming increasingly precise and flavorfully distinct as she practiced what she learned from classes at the Ecole Chocolat in Vancouver and Chicago's Callebaut Academy. After 20 years of gifting chocolate to friends, in 2016, she took her truffles retail in Sebastopol's former train station turned boutique marketplace, Gravenstein Station.

Two years later, Jill McLewis came aboard. Through her years as a critical care respiratory therapist, McLewis had always felt a tug toward pastry and confections, honing her skills in classes at Paris's Le Cordon Bleu and with the late Belgian master chocolatier Jean-Pierre Wybauw.

Step inside the tiny shop—about 20 candy boxes square—that manages to house both the commercial kitchen and retail area. Preservative-free candies are made with fresh purees, organic cream, and Belgian and French chocolate. Forty different flavors are available; the Orange Tuaca truffle, flavored with Italian brandy liquor, vanilla, and citrus, took Best of Show in the candy division at the 2020 Harvest Fair. Each candy is hand crafted, distinctively

Left: *Shop exterior*

Center top: *Candies are decorated according to flavor.*

Center above: *Salt-dusted caramels*

Top right: *Partners Sonja Schluter (left), Jill McLewis (right)*

Above right: *Candies come in 40 possible flavors. All photos courtesy Eye Candy*

molded, and decorated according to its flavor. Flavors are distinct yet never overwhelm; interiors are melt-in-the-mouth luscious inside a crisp but never brittle exterior. Packaging is jewel-box perfect. All are created, as the truffle-making duo say, "with laughter, care, and passion."

6761 Sebastopol Ave., Sebastopol, 707-888-0568
eyecandychocolatier.com

A portion of Eye Candy's proceeds benefit the Glaucoma Research Foundation.

EPICUREAN CONNECTION

You, too, can be a cheesemaker

Class begins with a glass of wine and a tasting of artisan cheeses and ends with participants heading out the door carrying a wheel of crème de ricotta they created themselves. With a recipe, ladle, cheesecloth, and cheese mold to get them started, they also leave confident that they can re-create the experience at home. In Epicurean Connection's kitchen classroom, chef Sheana Davis has made the process both fun and easy.

Davis's Epicurean Connection roots run deep in the Sonoma Valley. She was born and raised in Boyes Hot Springs, and her grandfather, a professional chef, allowed her to watch him cook in his kitchen and occasionally stir. By fourth grade she was canning vegetables from his garden. A teenaged Davis served as apprentice chef for M. F. K. Fisher at the famous food writer's "Last House" in Glen Ellen. As for Davis's cheesemaking skills, she credits the late, legendary Sonoma cheesemaker Ig Vella as teacher and mentor. One of his cheese knives and signature paper hats hang framed in her office.

Straight out of high school, Davis headed to Santa Rosa Junior College to enroll in culinary arts. After graduation, she opened Epicurean Connection, a café in a Boyes Hot Springs building where her grandfather had cooked years before.

When the café outgrew its location, a "new" Epicurean Connection moved to downtown Sonoma as a lunch and dinner café, beer and wine bar, and showcase for artisan and farmstead cheeses, with space for Davis's cheesemaking experimentations. In 2009, she released her first cheese, Delice de la Vallee; in 2010, the American Cheese Society named it the best fresh cheese in the country.

Top left: *Cheesemaking set up ready to go*

Above left: *Cheesemaking class awaiting instruction*

Center: *Chef and cheesemaker Sheana Davis*

Right: *All photos courtesy Sonoma County Tourism*

In September 2015, Davis sold the downtown location to open a newly imagined Epicurean Connection in an industrial park on the southeast edge of town focused on cheese production, cheesemaking classes, cooking classes, and catering.

On Friday and Saturday mornings, the shop opens with a fresh and local menu of prepared foods, fresh cheeses, meats, and dry grocery products.

19670 Eighth St. E, Sonoma, 707-235-9530
theepicureanconnection.com

Jay-Z and Beyoncé are among Delice de la Vallee's afficionados.

FARMHOUSE INN

Michelin-starred

When brother and sister Joe and Catherine Bartolomei, fifth-generation Sonoma farmers, bought a nearby 1873 farmhouse surrounded by eight workers' cottages, it wasn't much to look at. "Dilapidated," they describe their 2001 purchase. Nevertheless, from day one they saw potential.

Today their Farmhouse Inn is a super-luxurious yet laid-back wine-country getaway, named by international publications as one of the best boutique hotels in the world and top hotels in the United States. The centerpiece of the inn is its restaurant, which is no slouch in accumulating its own "bests," among them best restaurants in America, top 10 culinary inns, and America's most romantic restaurants. Not to mention the restaurant's 15 straight years of garnering a Michelin star under chef Steve Litke's kitchen leadership.

From his first days on the job, Litke set about forging strong relationships with local farmers and artisanal food producers, creating ever-changing seasonal menus to showcase their products. What emerged from the kitchen depended on what they had ready for harvesting. One of Litke's favorites, a menu staple from the start, was a simple salad constructed of what he describes as "absolutely the best greens grown in the county" that he'd pick up—washed and ready—on his way to the Farmhouse.

Litke's "rabbit, rabbit, rabbit" also appeared early on and stayed. Inspired by an appetizer at an Italian East Coast restaurant where he'd worked during the early years of his career, the rabbit was prepared three ways, as a confit leg, applewood-smoked bacon-wrapped loin, and small rack. Diners loved it.

Top left: *Lamb, perfectly cooked*

Above left: *Catherine and Joe Bartolomei, Farmhouse Inn co-owners*

Center: *Michelin star chef Steve Litke*

Top right: *Farmhouse Inn retains its 1873 farmhouse exterior.*

Above right: *Beautifully plated dishes emerge from the kitchen. All photos courtesy Sonoma County Tourism*

From the start, the Bartolomeis felt that if the restaurant blossomed, everything else they had in mind for their inn would follow. After 22 years, Litke announced what he calls his semi-retirement, catering exclusive, private-dining experiences for select clients. Moving into the Farmhouse kitchen is Chef Daniel Beal, former sous chef at San Francisco's three-Michelin-star Atelier Crenn. Says Litke, "I can't wait to see what Farmhouse does next. Whatever it is, I know it will be great."

7871 River Rd., Forestville, 707-887-3300
farmhouseinn.com

The Farmhouse Inn's dining room decor includes chandeliers made from wine barrel staves.

DON JULIO'S LATIN GRILL AND PUPUSAS

El Salvador's national dish

"Flatten it out, throw it on the grill, let it cook for about seven minutes on each side, and let all the stuff inside melt together." That's a pupusa, according to Carlos Alas Grande, whose parents opened Don Julio's in 2014. Carlos, now co-owner with his brother Cesar, heads the kitchen, but all the Alas Grandes pitch in as they have since opening day.

The family moved from El Salvador when Carlos was two years old. As a high schooler, he shared his mother Evelyn's pupusas with friends, who requested more. Evelyn's Salvadoran cookery led to Don Julio's opening. While Evelyn's original recipes have stretched into a menu that incorporates adaptations of Mexican favorites, the pupusas, El Salvador's national dish, are the star.

The slap, slap, slap of masa being turned into a filled tortilla patty has been heard in El Salvador for nearly 2,000 years. Archaeologists have unearthed cooking tools and pupusa ingredients at numerous digging sites, among them Joya de Cerén, El Salvador's "Pompeii," an ancient village buried by a volcanic eruption. The earliest versions were vegetarian half-moons (meat

On every second Sunday in November, El Salvador celebrates National Pupusa Day in honor of its national dish, with pupusa-eating contests and attempts to shatter the 2015 Guinness World Record of a pupusa nearly 15 feet in diameter.

Top left: *Pupusa burger, an Alas Grande innovation. Photo courtesy Sonoma County Tourism*

Above left: *Restaurant's logo reflects the family's Salvadoran roots. Photo courtesy Yvonne Horn*

Top right: *The entire Alas Grande family pitches in to run the restaurant. Photo courtesy Don Julio's*

Above right: *Don Julio's modest but colorfully Salvadoran interior. Photo courtesy Yvonne Horn*

was not added until 1570); today's pupusas are full moons, stuffed with mild cheese and meat or vegetarian options. Grilled until puffy and speckled with brown, they are always accompanied by garlic and onions, tomato salsa, and *curtido*, a crunchy fermented slaw of cabbage and carrots flavored with onion.

Between bites, sip a mango-pineapple agua fresca and you'll be in Salvadoran heaven.

217 Southwest Blvd., Rohnert Park, 707-242-3160
donjulioslatingrill.com

HANA

A true taste of Japan

Snag a seat at the sushi bar and be transported from an unassuming Rohnert Park strip mall to Tokyo Bay. Make your choice from suggestions on the board or just point; you won't be disappointed. Anything passed across the counter will be a piece of art created from the best and freshest raw fish in the world, mouthwateringly delicious. For 30 years, chef-owner Ken Tominaga has overseen perfection, often crafting his signature specialties alongside the other chefs behind the counter.

But there's more to be had at Hana than impeccable sushi; the traditional Japanese dishes are equally fresh and delicious.

Tominaga grew up in Tokyo with parents who immersed their son in the city's dining scene. As a teenager, Tominaga became part of that scene as a dishwasher, moving up to prep cook, then scurrying home to catch a few hours of sleep before school. While his parents didn't discourage his culinary ambitions, the family's business was optics, a business that, it so happened, had a presence in Santa Rosa. When Tominaga's schooling was complete, he came to Sonoma County to join the family's enterprise. Quickly he began to explore the area's wealth of cuisines: French, Italian, Chinese, American, and more. All set his taste buds tingling. "One foot in Tokyo, one foot in Northern California," he describes it.

The opportunity to return to his homeland's cuisine came when his family sold their business. He enrolled in Tokyo's

Dustin Valette, chef-owner of the Matheson, called in Ken Tominaga to collaborate on the design and set-up of his restaurant's sushi kitchen.

Top left: *Sushi counter*

Above left: *Tokyo-inspired menu items*

Top right: *Impeccably fresh seafood from sushi bar*

Above right: *Chef Ken Tominaga. All photos courtesy Hana*

Akasaka Cooking School, learning to master classic dishes by day and frequenting sushi restaurants at night. Sushi masters that he had known as a boy shared tips and recipes that he began to merge into his personal yet traditional style.

Tominaga views his restaurant as a daily learning process, never resting on Hana's laurels as one of the Bay Area's leading Japanese restaurants. Ingredients are impeccable; fish are flown in daily from Tokyo or locally sourced. Staff are trained to gently guide diners in how best to eat and enjoy traditional Japanese cuisine.

Under sake sommelier Danny Pitassy, diners are invited to explore Hana's extensive list of sakes. Japanese beers and compatible wines are also available.

101 Golf Course Dr., Rohnert Park, 707-586-0270
hanajapanese.com

SANTA ROSA SEAFOOD

Straight from the sea

Ice-layered counters display seafood just hours out of the sea. Albacore tuna, lingcod, salmon, and halibut pulled out of Bodega Bay are nestled next to mahi mahi flown in overnight from Hawaii, orange roughy from New Zealand, fish from the Gulf, and East Coast lobster. Or choose from a dozen or so varieties of oysters and clams.

Mike Svedise and his wife, Trudy, started it all. Mike was born with sea water in his veins into an extended three-generation Italian family of North Bay San Francisco fishermen. As a kid, he'd cut school at every opportunity to hide out on his uncle's boat and spend the day happily fishing. In 1976, he bought his first commercial fishing boat, unloading its catch on Fisherman's Wharf, where Trudy ran a tackle shop.

Twenty years and four children later, the couple had progressed from Trudy's tackle shop and Mike's one boat to a small fleet of boats operating out of Bodega Bay, their catch sold at stands in 16 of the area's farmers markets—all the while dreaming of owning a wholesale/retail store. In 2002, it happened. Santa Rosa Seafood opened in a 6,000-square-foot building with sufficient adjacent space for a seafood restaurant to come later. The entire family pitched in, including children Sal, Nick, Joe, and Anna.

Anna Svedise struck out on her own with Anna's Seafood in Petaluma.

901 Lakeville St., Petaluma, 707-664-5074
shopannasseafood.com

Left: *Anna Svedise. Photo courtesy Anna's Seafood*

Center: *Catch fresh out of Bodega Bay. Photo courtesy Anna's Seafood*

Top right: *Seafood fills ice-layered counters. Photo courtesy Yvonne Horn*

Above right: *Trudy and Mike Svedise. Photo courtesy Santa Rosa Seafood*

In 2017, the unthinkable happened. At the age of 59, Mike Svedise unexpectedly died. Devastated beyond measure, the Svedises carried on.

In addition to counters filled with an impressive choice of seasonal seafood, count on ready-to-carry-home cartons of clam chowder and rich, delicious cioppino. A line of customers will be waiting to pick up the family's trademarked "smoasted" salmon. Roasted and smoked in wood-fired ovens adjacent to the store, fillets emerge with just a whisper of smoke enhancing the mahogany glazed salmon's succulent interior. Enjoy with no fuss or muss. A squeeze of lemon is all that's needed.

946 Santa Rosa Ave., Santa Rosa, 707-579-2085
santarosaseafood.com

THE SEA RANCH LODGE

At one with the sea and the land

In the 1960s, a spectacular 10-mile-long, 7,000-acre stretch of wave-dashed rocky coves along Highway 1 became a coastal community—the Sea Ranch. Designed by a cadre of environmentally minded architects with "living lightly on the land" as their mantra, strict architectural rules included sloping roofs, unpainted siding, no fences, native vegetation as plantings, and cypress hedgerows to tame the winds. Timeless, unpretentious. So it remains today, with 2,200 houses unassumingly settled into the meadows and hills straddling the highway.

The Sea Ranch Lodge, one of the community's most architecturally notable and iconic structures, recently emerged from a two-year renovation. With little change to the exterior, interior spaces were reimagined to create a simpler and more open plan, with areas better connected visually to the lodge's meadow and ocean setting. Sea Ranchers celebrated in the reopening of what they consider to be their community's hub and social center.

Choose any seat in the dining room and you'll have a panoramic view. Executive Chef Eric Piacentine follows suit with dishes inspired by land and sea. "It's exciting to work with local farmers, fishermen, and foragers to create a fresh new menu that complements this beautiful place where land meets sea," he says. Piacentine defines what emerges from his kitchen as "rugged, refined dining." Think Sonoma duck with wild rice, beets, and huckleberries or house-made pappardelle pasta with foraged mushrooms.

Piacentine's passion for cooking began far from the sea—in his family-owned bakeries and bread shops around Wisconsin. After attending culinary school in Florida, he apprenticed under a private chef. Venturing out West, he worked in a number of kitchens,

Top left: *Houses designed to rest lightly on the land. Photo courtesy Sonoma County Tourism*

Above left: *Lodge exterior. Photo courtesy The Sea Ranch Lodge/Carlos Chavarria*

Top center: *Chef Eric Piacentina. Photo courtesy The Sea Ranch Lodge/Stephanie Russo*

Above center: *Bar bites. Photo courtesy The Sea Ranch Lodge/Stephanie Russo*

Right: *Dishes inspired by land and sea. Photo courtesy The Sea Ranch Lodge/Stephanie Russo*

including at the one-Michelin-starred Boulevard in San Francisco and as executive sous chef at the acclaimed Bernardus Lodge in Carmel Valley. Given his Wisconsin bakery roots, expect stand-out desserts ranging from a local Gravenstein apple galette to sweet and savory donuts with assorted dipping sauces.

60 Sea Walk Dr., Sea Ranch, 707-579-9777
thesearanchlodge.com

Renovated guest rooms will be ready for occupancy in 2023.

STORMY'S SPIRITS & SUPPER

One of the county's oldest

Bloomfield, mid-1850s: the county's second-largest town. It thrived as a major stagecoach stop, with a population of 350. (The population was more likely 800 to 1,000, researchers say, as census records from that time didn't cover everyone. Only white adult males were counted, no women, no Chinese immigrants, no Native Americans.)

Stagecoach passengers by the dozens stopped off to have a meal or stay the night at the Big Valley Inn, with three additional hotels slated for opening. And then came the railroad, but not to Bloomfield. Bypassed by train travel, bustling Bloomfield dwindled. The 2021 census accurately listed 292 Bloomfield souls.

As for the Big Valley Inn, since 1961 the redwood- and stone-clad roadhouse has been known as Stormy's. Ellen Cramer—nickname Stormy—bought the place and for a time ran it as a bar, serving snacks and sandwiches. In the early 1970s, her son Roger, who'd been sweeping floors and stocking cans of beer and soda since he was 11, turned Stormy's into a steakhouse. With Roger in the kitchen and his wife, Carolyn, and daughter, Taylor Marie, involved, the three-generation Cramer family has operated the roadhouse longer than any other owners in its nearly 170-year history.

The dining room is cozy, but regulars head for the bar, where a year-round fireplace provides welcoming warmth from evening fogs creeping in from the nearby coast. Although other items are listed on the menu—chicken and seafood, for example—decades of regulars have come solely for Stormy's house-aged steaks and Roger's signature prime rib au jus. Roger has been known to march around

Top left: *Highway sign announces Bloomfield. Photo courtesy Yvonne Horn*

Above left: *Stormy's redwood and stone 1881 exterior. Photo courtesy Sonoma County Tourism*

Top right: *Entrance sign for Stormy's, in the Cramer family since 1961. Photo courtesy Sonoma County Tourism*

Above right: *Since 1961, the historic inn has been known as Stormy's. Photo courtesy Sonoma County Tourism*

the dining room proudly showing off a perfectly cooked prime rib in its giant roasting pan. All beef portions, whether steaks or prime rib, are enormous, with a "regular cut" weighing in at 22 to 24 ounces and the smaller "side kick" at 16. Everything on the menu comes with clam chowder, a green salad, buttermilk mashed potatoes, a vegetable, and French bread. It makes for a comfort-food monster meal. Most customers heading out the door have a doggy box in hand.

6650 Bloomfield Rd., Petaluma, 707-795-0127
stormysrestaurant.com

Along with Stormy's, two other buildings remain from Bloomfield's bustling days: the Masonic Hall and the "town hall," once the Odd Fellows Hall and now occupied by the volunteer fire department.

TABLE CULTURE PROVISIONS

Comfort food plus

Ask for directions, and you'll be told that Table Culture Provisions is across the street from Pinky's Pizza Parlor. That helps. Pinky's is very pink and very large. Table Culture Provisions is very small, painted dark green, with only its name etched into the glass front door letting you know you've arrived. But once you've found it, you'll be back again and again.

When chef-owners Stéphane Saint Louis and Steven Vargas launched their restaurant in 2022, they were known entities. Pop-ups had created a buzz among foodies that the duo was turning out crave-worthy cookery. Comforting standards like burgers emerged with panache. Special dinners offered French classics and a Haitian feast.

A Haitian feast? Saint Louis was born in New York and raised in Haiti. Arriving in Northern California in his late teens, he enrolled in San Francisco's California Culinary Academy. After working in several restaurants in the United States, wanderlust took him to France, where he studied at the Institut Paul Bocuse before stints in such far-flung places as Copenhagen and Shanghai. Adding to Table Culture Provisions's international flair, Saint Louis's wife, Marta, who heads the front of the house, grew up in Poland, where she graduated from the Hospitality and Culinary Institute.

Vargas, on the other hand, was born and raised in Petaluma and never strayed far. Interested more in sports than time in front of a stove, his appreciation for professional cookery began while working with Chef Ricky Garcia at Dinucci's in Valley Ford. That led to the Santa Rosa Junior College's Culinary Arts Program. After finishing

Top left: *Restaurant street view. Photo courtesy Sonoma County Tourism*

Above left: *The final touch. Photo courtesy Table Culture Provisions*

Right: *Stéphane Saint Louis (right) and Steven Vargas (left) co-chefs and owners. Photo courtesy Table Culture Provisions*

the program, his first job was at Della Fattoria, where Saint Louis was working. The two worked well together. When Saint Louis suggested a joint restaurant venture, Vargas, who considers Saint Louis a mentor and brother, found it an easy decision.

The duo's journey toward eatery ownership hit a rocky road during the pandemic. As a last resort, they invested their stimulus checks in electric car company Tesla, resulting in a $17,000 windfall that put them on the way to their destination, Table Culture Provisions.

312 Petaluma Blvd. S, Petaluma, 707-559-5739
tcprovision.com

"My favorite type of food is simple but elevated through technique and quality of ingredients." –Chef Steven Vargas

THE MADRONA

Inspired by the garden

John Alexander Paxton built his mansion overlooking Dry Creek Valley in 1881 for $12,000, all 17 rooms, four baths, and seven fireplaces of it. It remained a private home for 100 years, until purchased by John Harry Muir, who turned it into a country inn, Madrona Manor. In 1999, Trudi and Bill Konrad bought the property, remarketing the inn as a romantic getaway and bringing in chef Jesse Mallgren to head the kitchen.

Like so many of Sonoma County's notable chefs, Mallgren's career began as a dishwasher, moving on to work with such esteemed chefs as Gary Danko, then with Chateau Souverain in Geyserville, and Jeremiah Tower at San Francisco's legendary Stars. The Konrads gave Mallgren full rein, with Michelin awarding Madrona Manor a star for 13 consecutive years. For inspiration, Mallgren looked to the manor's organic vegetable gardens and orchard, with the goal that every menu item contain at least one "of-the-moment ingredient." As for the mansion, it remained steeped in Victorian flavor; for years the Konrads hosted holiday Dickens Dinners with costumed carolers and rooms lavishly filled with trees and toys.

In the spring of 2021, following purchase by a San Francisco investment group, Madrona Mansion closed its doors. One year

"When you see perfect fruit on the tree or pluck a cherry tomato still warm from the sun, how can you not want to rush back to the kitchen?" –Chef Jesse Mallgren

Left: *Exterior of 1881 mansion, now the Madrona. All photos courtesy The Madrona*
Right: *Chef Jesse Mallgren in the estate's garden*

later, it reopened as the Madrona, the 19th-century belle turned stylish with a light and airy redo by San Francisco designer Jay Jeffers. Instead of throwing Victoriana to the wind, Jeffers incorporated furnishings and artwork from the manor's past into each room.

In contrast to Madrona Manor's reputation as a sought-out, special-occasion place, Mallgren now oversees a kitchen with a more casual a la carte menu. A complete dining experience can be had in the dining room or on the terrace; a limited menu and drinks are available on the wrap-around porch, in the front parlor, and in Hannah's Bar (named for the original owner's wife, Hannah Paxton). Mallgren describes the new dining experience as familiar and approachable, yet inspired, as before, by what is fresh and seasonal in the estate's garden.

1001 Westside Rd., Healdsburg, 707-395-6700
themadronahotel.com

VINOMA TAPAS ARGENTINAS

From bouquets to empanadas

Who can resist when *Sonoma Magazine* lists a place in a service station as one of the best eateries you've never heard of? Pull into the Shell gas station minutes off roaring Highway 101 and fill up on Vinoma's empanadas in a space once occupied by a Subway shop. It's an order-at-the-counter sort of place. While there are several small tables with chairs out front and a bit of seating inside, most customers consider it a grab-and-go. Congratulations if you make it home with no crumbs to brush off your shirt; it's hard to resist eating chef Brian Corrigan's empanadas fresh out of the oven right now.

One option is to bring them home frozen. As Corrigan directs, heat your oven to 410 degrees, line a sheet pan with parchment paper, and bake for 20 to 25 minutes, peeking now and then to see if they are nicely browned. Allow them to cool a bit before biting straight into Argentina. Although empanadas aren't the country's national dish—that would be *asado*, an assortment of meats grilled on a wood-fired *parrilla*—empanadas come close.

Half-rounds of crimped-edged, flaky pastry are filled with a variety of fillings; Vinoma thoughtfully initials the crust of each so you can tell which of what you've brought home. Savory meat fillings, such as the carne picante (beef sauteed with red bell

The name Vinoma is a combination of the names of the couple's children.

Top left: *Boxed canastitas and empanadas*

Above left: *Little bouquets top each boxed order*

Right: *Chef/owner Brian Corrigan. All photos courtesy Vinomas Tapas Argentinas*

peppers, onions, and hot paprika), are traditional, but Vinoma also offers vegetarian possibilities like choclo a la crema (sweet corn, onion, garlic, nutmeg, and cream sauce). Canastitas, or "little baskets," are also on the menu; they are open-faced mini-pies with similar fillings. All are house made from scratch, from rolling out the dough to mixing the fillings.

Growing up on the East Coast, Corrigan entered the restaurant scene as a teenage dishwasher, working his way up through the years to chef positions. Credit his wife, Lorena Bresso, of Italian descent but born and raised in Argentina, as Vinoma's inspiration. As a finishing touch, each order is topped by a small bouquet of flowers picked daily from the family's Sebastopol home garden.

5085 Redwood Dr., Rohnert Park, 707-536-9215
vinoma.net

LIGHTWAVE CAFÉ

Monte Rio's reimagined café

On sunny mornings, locals stop by to chat over coffee at umbrella-shaded picnic benches out front. A few well-mannered dogs wander about. Attached to the café, a deck filled with small tables overlooks a tennis court, community garden, and skateboard park. All are part of what used to be Monte Rio's elementary school campus and is now Creekside Park. Redwood-covered hills encircle it all.

To say "Lightwave Café" is to say Ori and Gal—literally. Ori translates from the Hebrew as "my light," Gal as "wave." Born, raised, and married in Jerusalem, Ori and Gal Ginzburg's presence in Monte Rio came about via an involved and circuitous route where the Ginzburgs found themselves working on a Valley Ford chicken ranch. Several days a week, Ori also helped the owner of the café, then a vegan spot. Business was slow, and the owner wanted out. Might the Ginzburgs be interested? It was a momentous decision, but after considering that café ownership encompassed what they like best to do—be among people, host them, and feed them—they took a leap of faith.

Their café's tiny interior is just big enough to step into and place an order. Even so, one wants to linger. Every inch of wall space is lined or hung with memorabilia—old photos, knickknacks, weathered teapots, and an impressive number of radios from times gone by. Skateboards hung on the door to the deck are whimsically painted.

Classic Israeli dishes are on the menu—beach laffa, shakshuka, and bourekas, for example—all beautifully presented, enticingly flavored, and enhanced by Israeli music wafting softly from the kitchen. Ingredients are fresh, and dishes are cooked to order.

Top left: *Jars of pickles for sale*

Above left: *Café exterior*

Center top: *Bourekas plate*

Center above: *Gal Ginzburg*

Right: *Ori (left) and Gal Ginzburg. All photos courtesy Lightwave Café*

When asked how and where they learned to cook, the Ginzburgs chorus "grandmama"—watching and helping their respective grandmothers prepare the foods that they grew up with and that now emerge from Lightwave's kitchen.

Both are cooks and do the prep work together. When the café opens, Ori becomes front of the house, welcoming eaters, taking orders, and delivering drinks; Gal runs the kitchen. Ori says that Gal is the "palate" of the two, the decisionmaker on seasoning matters. He refers to her as "the chef."

9725 Main St., Monte Rio, 707-865-5169
lightwavecafe.square.site

The Ginzburgs' pickles are so loved that the café sells them by the jar labeled Zois & Zissel, meaning "sweet and salty" in Yiddish.

GYPSY CAFÉ

Fueling the soul

It was time for refurbishment, actually past time; the beloved Pine Cone Café had been serving substantial breakfasts and lunches to the Sebastopol community for close to 50 years. Shawn E. Hall, an interior designer specializing in the hospitality industry, was hired for the job. Walls were gutted, exposing the original building's weathered brick and old timber interior, and a new kitchen was installed. Hall was then asked whether she could help find a new owner.

During her career, Hall had breathed new life into dozens of tired eateries. "I get into a space, find its bones, bring it to life, and then walk away," she says. This time she didn't walk away. In 2011, she bought the Pine Cone and opened the Gypsy Café.

The word gypsy pays homage to Hall's mother, a single mom who supported herself and her daughter by renovating houses. "We lived in 13 houses in eight years," she says. Her mother, an adopted orphan, never knew her cultural roots. Hall set out on a quest to find them, bringing back from her travels wanderlust remnants that she merged into the café's decor—old signage, antiques, and ornate mirrors—rustic salvage at its best, mixed in with colorful abstract art. Weathered doors became repurposed into the café's decor, harking back to Hall's amazement when her mother created a table out of one.

Other items have been gifted by customers; take notice of the framed, crocheted pineapple (a symbol of hospitality) brought in on the café's first anniversary and the "Draperies" sign hanging over the bar from a grateful couple who collects antiques.

While the café's decor fuels the imagination, what Hall refers to as "modern comfort food" fuels the soul with made-from-scratch offerings for breakfast and lunch, as well as brunch on Sundays.

Top left: *Owner Shawn E. Hall seated at the counter. Photo courtesy Gypsy Café*

Above left: *General Store. Photo courtesy Gypsy Café*

Top right: *Gypsy Café interior. Photo courtesy Sonoma County Tourism*

Above right: *Repurposed decor throughout the café. Photo courtesy Gypsy Café*

Dinners happen on the first Friday of each month. Live music enlivens the scene as diners tuck into such favorites as Gypsy pot roast—beef braised in red wine and served over polenta.

162 N Main St., Sebastopol, 707-861-3825
gypsy-cafe.com

A colorful beach umbrella hung upside down from the ceiling identifies a small space set aside as the General Store, which displays handmade goods such as pillows, olive-wood bowls, hand-painted pottery, placemats, and the café's signature Gypsy waffle mix.

CUMIN

Faraway flavors

The staff of *Sonoma Magazine* worked as a team to assemble "The 50 Best Things to Eat in Sonoma County" for the summer 2021 issue, a list of dishes and the best places to order them. Among them was Cumin's butter chicken, described as "shredded dark meat chicken in a delicately spiced tomato sauce that when served with garlic naan is as comforting as a warm hug." Readers paid attention, and butter chicken flew off Cumin's extensive menu of over 100 items spanning the cuisines of Nepal, India, and Tibet.

Rak Thapa and his partner, Dhiraj Kafle, successful owners of restaurants for over 20 years, opened Cumin in 2019, moving into a space in the small, tucked-away, upscale Sunrise Plaza, a space that had seen other restaurants quickly come and go. In the kitchen, two self-trained chefs were turning out cuisine inspired by the foods they grew up with in the foothills of the Himalayas and in India's cities. Even before hitting the "50 Best" list, Cumin looked good to stay in Sunrise Plaza, with a menu attracting notice for its unusual dishes and nuanced sauces.

It survived even when, with no fanfare or notice, Cumin changed ownership in the fall of 2021. Without missing a beat, Shrija Thapa (no relation to Rak Thapa; Thapa is a common Nepalese name) was now the owner. The same cooks continue manning the kitchen, with customer favorites such as aloo gobi, tandoor-baked spinach naan, and yes, butter chicken emerging exactly as before.

Shrija Thapa came to the United States as a student. Before continuing to Texas, where she'd be studying, she stopped in Petaluma to visit a friend. It was to Sonoma County that she returned, now married, working in a Petaluma grocery store but

Top left: *Shrija Thapa owner, left, and sister Shreya Thapa. Photo courtesy Yvonne Horn*

Above left: *Peas pulav. Photo courtesy Cumin Restaurant*

Top right: *Aloo gobi. Photo courtesy Cumin Restaurant*

Above right: *Exterior. Photo courtesy Yvonne Horn*

wanting something different to do. At the same time, a family necessity was calling Rak Thapa back to Nepal. Serendipity happened.

Shreya Thapa joined her sister to help run Cumin with but two changes: Shrija adjusted some spices to reflect her palate, and little bouquets of flowers now center the tables.

170 Farmers Ln., Suite 8, Santa Rosa, 707-771-8336
cuminsantarosa.com

SingleThread

An *omotenashi* experience

Sonoma County immediately took notice when Kyle and Katina Connaughton's SingleThread opened its doors in 2017. As did Michelin, describing the dining experience a mere year after the restaurant's opening as "exquisite" and awarding it two stars. The following year, Michelin deemed SingleThread three-star worthy, with "exceptional cuisine worth a special journey."

An evening at SingleThread is a *kaiseki* parade, each course a culinary and artistic masterpiece. Dishes appear on handcrafted ceramics; lighting and soft music are engineered to discreetly change as the meal progresses. Service is *omotenashi*, "the spirit of selfless hospitality, anticipating needs without being asked." Plan on four hours—and a well-stacked wallet—to savor the experience.

Intrinsic to the culinary excellence is the restaurant's nearby five-acre farm, tended by Katina and her team of SingleThread gardeners. Production focuses on what can't be found elsewhere in the region—lily bulbs and Japanese carrots, for example; flowers and foliage become enchanting floral arrangements.

Kyle and Katina grew up in Southern California and have known each other since they were 15. Kyle remembers his first excursion into Japanese food—the unforgettable taste and textures of sushi—at age nine. While still in high school he apprenticed at one of the oldest Japanese restaurants in Southern California. Through the years, his deepening appreciation and understanding of the cuisine came about through hands-on cooking with traditional Japanese chefs, culminating with several years spent with famed chef Michel Bras in Hokkaido.

Katina's foray into farming began during their time in Hokkaido and continued in Sonoma during the years she and Kyle

Left: *Fine dining with exquisite finishing touches. Photo courtesy Sonoma County Tourism*

Top center: *SingleThread fine-dining experience. Photo courtesy Sonoma County Tourism/ John Trafell*

Above center: *SingleThread restaurant viewed from the street. Photo courtesy Sonoma County Tourism*

Right: *Chef Kyle Connaughton with wife Katina on their SingleThread farm. Photo courtesy Sonoma County Tourism*

spent planning and working out every detail of the restaurant and farm they had in mind. She completed coursework in sustainable agriculture and horticulture, worked in the Santa Rosa Junior College's greenhouse, and farmed at several winery properties.

SingleThread's logo, adorning everything from chef coats to the signage outside the restaurant, is the image of an onion flower. "The onion is the only vegetable that can be grown on the farm and served in the restaurant the year around," Kyle and Katina explain. "It's the single thread that connects everything."

131 North St., Healdsburg, 707-723-4646
singlethreadfarms.com

Extend your Michelin-starred *omotenashi* experience with an overnight stay in one of SingleThread's five guest rooms.

FARMERS MARKETS

Bounty of the county

When Hilda Swartz, now into her 80s, began managing farmers markets, there were but three in the county—Santa Rosa, Healdsburg, and Sonoma. That was in 1985. At last count, there are 28, some year-round, others operating seasonally.

Swartz continuous to manage two of them—one, in the town of Sonoma, is among the county's largest; the second, in Santa Rosa's Oakmont Village, is the smallest. Swartz easily lays claim to being Sonoma County's longest-serving farmers market manager.

It's not easy work. While managers newer to the job than Swartz undoubtedly use computers to keep track of "paperwork," hers *is* on paper, in the thick notebooks she keeps for each of her markets. There are vendor fees to keep track of, applications, certification requirements, agricultural and health department rules and inspections, and more. "That's the least enjoyable part of what I do," she says. "What I love is talking with the shoppers and working with my vendors, the best in the world!"

Sonoma County at the turn of the 20th century was known as San Francisco's market basket. It remains an important market basket today, even as wine grapes have taken center stage. An increasing number of small farmers remain dedicated to providing the quality ingredients that fuel memorable restaurant meals and locals' kitchens. Farmers markets showcase it all.

"In my years as a manager, I've overseen generations of vendors. Some I held on my lap as children are selling now." –Hilda Swartz

Top left: *Bounty of the county. Photo courtesy Sonoma County Tourism*

Above left: *Seasonal fresh produce. Photo courtesy Farm Trails*

Top center: *Produce-filled stall. Photo courtesy Sonoma County Tourism*

Right: *Hilda Swartz with vendor's son. Photo courtesy Yvonne Horn*

Instagram-worthy displays of fruits and vegetables abound throughout the seasons, but stalls are also filled with honey, eggs, cheese, meats and seafood, breads and pastries, flowers and seedlings, and artisan crafts. At some markets, music by homegrown talent plays in the background. As you fill your market basket, rub elbows with chefs in search of menu inspiration, chat with other shoppers, and become acquainted with those who produce the abundance—it's an oh-so-Sonoma County thing to do.

farmtrails.org/farmers-markets

Café Aquatica
Courtesy Café Aquatica

EATS AND EATERIES A-Z

Tasca Tasca
Courtesy Tasca Tasca/
Erik Castro Photography

Table Culture Provisions
Courtesy Table Culture Provisions

APPENDIX

The Sea Ranch Lodge
Courtesy The Sea Ranch Lodge/Stephanie Russo

Barndiva
Courtesy Barndiva